Authority and the Church

AUTHORITY AND THE CHURCH

Papers and Discussions at
a Conference between theologians
of the Church of England and the
German Evangelical Church

EDITED BY

R. R. WILLIAMS

Bishop of Leicester

LONDON

S·P·C·K

1965

First published in 1965
by S.P.C.K.
Holy Trinity Church
Marylebone Road
London N.W.1

Printed in Great Britain by
The Talbot Press (S.P.C.K.)
Saffron Walden, Essex

CONTENTS

1*

LIST OF DELEGATES

The Evangelical Church in Germany

Professor Dr HEINRICH GREEVEN
  Professor of New Testament, Kiel.

Professor Dr ERNST KASEMANN
  Professor of New Testament, Tübingen.

Professor Dr ERNST KINDER
  Professor of Systematic Theology, Münster.

Professor Dr MARTIN SCHMIDT
  Professor of Church History, Mainz.

Professor Dr WOLFGANG SCHWEITZER
  Professor of Systematic Theology, Bethel.

The Church of England

The Right Reverend R. R. WILLIAMS (Chairman)
  Bishop of Leicester.

The Reverend Canon J. ATKINSON
  Lecturer in Theology, Hull. (Theological Secretary)

The Reverend Canon S. L. GREENSLADE
  Regius Professor of Ecclesiastical History, Oxford.

The Reverend Canon G. W. H. LAMPE
  Ely Professor of Divinity, Cambridge.

The Reverend Canon C. F. D. MOULE
  Lady Margaret's Professor of Divinity, Cambridge.

The Reverend Canon I. T. RAMSEY
  Nolloth Professor of Philosophy of Christian Religion, Oxford.

The Reverend Canon H. E. W. TURNER
  Van Mildert Professor of Divinity, Durham.

The Reverend Dr A. B. WILKINSON
  Chaplain of St Catharine's College, Cambridge.

Staff

The Reverend E. H. GORDON

The Reverend ECKHARD VON RABENAU

The Reverend H. G. ROENSTEIN

The Reverend DAVID TUSTIN

INTRODUCTION

In April, 1964, a Conference was held at Ripon Hall, Oxford, between representatives of the Church of England and representatives of the Evangelical Church of Germany. The list of delegates is printed on page vi.

The short speech that I made at the opening of the Conference will perhaps serve as a suitable Foreword to this volume, which records the main papers and contributions to the discussions. The German members of the Conference particularly asked that these words should be printed at the beginning of our Report.

I must, however, first, take this opportunity of saying what a stimulating experience it was for us Anglicans to share these few days of spiritual and intellectual fellowship with our German guests. All who took part look back with pleasure on the Conference, and look forward with hope to further contact in the future. A great debt of gratitude is due to the officials of the Church of England Council on Foreign Relations, in particular to the Reverend David Tustin, and to the Reverend E. H. Gordon, who undertook the heavy task of translating the German papers and other contributions.

No claim is made to have produced a full account of the lengthy discussions, conducted in English and German, and sometimes in unusual mixtures of both languages. What is recorded, however, will help to give readers some picture of the reactions of German and English delegates to the carefully prepared material of the papers.

Opening Speech

It is a great privilege which has fallen to me to preside over these few days of friendly and earnest theological discussion between theological scholars of the Church of England and similar scholars from the Evangelical or Lutheran Church of Germany.

This is no new contact between our Churches. There was, of course, a time when no organizational or doctrinal barrier separated us, the time of the medieval or pre-Reformation Church. Perhaps we in England feel our continuity with those days somewhat more strongly than do our fellow-Christians in the Lutheran Church—I suspect that rather more of our church buildings are medieval than yours, but that is an architectural accident, if it is true. But since the great upheaval of the sixteenth century, we have frequently been brought into contact. Our first Reformers at Cambridge owed much to their visits to Germany when it was under the strong influence of Luther himself. The music of Bach, much of it provided for the special benefit of Lutheran worship, has been increasingly valued in England, and much of it was heard this Easter, the Matthew Passion in my own Cathedral in Leicester. In 1841 we were in close touch over the setting up of a joint bishopric in Jerusalem. This lasted until 1886, when it became solely an Anglican responsibility.

The twentieth century has seen our countries twice tragically separated by war. During the Second World War some contact, however tenuous, was maintained through the ecumenical move-ment. The name of George Bell, formerly Bishop of Chichester, must be remembered in this connection.

Since the war, there has been much fellowship at different levels of Church life. The Cathedral at Coventry, rebuilt after the disaster of its destruction, has been the scene of much-valued help and fellowship from Christians in Germany. In the realm of theology, perhaps never before has there been so much influence from Germany. Barth and Brunner have yielded pride of place to Bultmann, and British scholars, no less than German, have ranged themselves for and against the great Marburg *Neutestamentler*.

Since the War of 1939-45 there have been various conferences, beginning in 1948 at Iserlohn, with a return conference at Oxford in 1949; one at Lambeth Palace in 1955; one at Münster in 1956, and one at Oxford in 1959. If there is a difference between our Conference and those that have preceded it, it is that official delegates have been appointed by the Church of England for this Conference, which takes place, as far as our Church of England is concerned, under the auspices of the Archbishop of Canterbury.

So we come to our little conference between a few English and a

few German scholars on the subject of "Authority and the Church".
"The question of authority, in its religious form," said P. T. Forsyth,
"is the first and last issue of life." Almost all theological questions
are wrapped up in this one. It includes the grounds on which we
believe at all; it includes the nature of Holy Scripture; authority in
the Church, and over the Church; the place of the Holy Spirit, of
tradition, and reason; the ministry, the nature of authority in the
sphere of moral action, and most important of all, the authority
of the Lord himself. We shall certainly not cover all this ground
this week. But as we exchange our thoughts on various aspects of
this subject we shall, by God's grace, get to know and understand
each other better, and enter more fully into the traditions whereby
our Churches have come to be what they are, and hence to make
us individually what we are.

———

Professor Wolfgang Schweitzer, leader of the German delegation, in
replying to my welcome, recalled that even before the First World
War a large-scale meeting with something like 130 members on
each side had taken place in this country between representatives of
the German Evangelical Churches and of the Church of England.
The prime mover on the German side at that time was Professor F.
Siegmund-Schultze, who subsequently founded the periodical *Die
Eiche* and made a great contribution to the movement which led,
after the War, to the founding of the World Alliance for Inter-
national Friendship through the Churches. It was agreed to send a
message of greeting to Professor Siegmund-Schultze.

Professor Schweitzer on behalf of the Evangelical Church in
Germany, expressed great satisfaction that this new series of
conversations had now come about, involving theologians officially
chosen to represent the two Churches concerned.

In a preliminary discussion it was pointed out that the English
word "authority" could be translated by two different German
words, *Autorität* and *Vollmacht*, both expressing different aspects
of the meaning of ἐξουσία. The German term *Vollmacht* means
literally "full power" and is used, for example, to describe the
power of attorney. It often refers to external and formalized
authority, meaning in effect "authorization"; whereas *Autorität*

often has the sense of the moral authority inherent in a person in virtue of his position or qualification.

The translation of ἐξουσία by the Latin term *auctoritas* had already shifted the emphasis in a legalistic direction, and such thinking had left its mark on the practice and thought of Western Christendom. However, as was said, in the New Testament ἐξουσία is not a problem—it is a fact in the person of Jesus Christ. It was generally agreed that the discussion of the term "authority" should not be restricted within the terms of the ecclesiastical hierarchy and its operations. The ultimate source of authority in the Church, it was felt, must be recognized as the Holy Spirit himself.

In the Final Session of the Conference, it was decided to publish an account of these discussions in English and German independently. It was also thought desirable that this series of conversations between the Evangelical Church in Germany and the Church of England should be continued, possibly at two-yearly intervals.

September 1964.   RONALD LEICESTER

PART ONE

The Authority of Scripture and Tradition

PAPER BY

CANON G. W. H. LAMPE

Since the first paper on this topic has been assigned to an Anglican,
I hope it will not be thought inappropriate to take as a starting-
point the statements about Scripture and Tradition that are contained in the Anglican formularies.

These sixteenth-century documents express what was at that
time a consistent and intelligible view of scriptural authority
common in all essentials to the Reformers in general, whether
English or Continental. This view was indeed by no means wholly
novel or revolutionary. The supreme, and indeed unique, authority
of Scripture had been consistently upheld by the Church in the
patristic period and the Middle Ages. But the nature of this
authority was now being understood and proclaimed in a new way.
There was a new emphasis upon the literal sense of the text, and a
new determination to read the Scriptures not simply as a convenient
collection of proof-texts available for the support of ecclesiastical
dogma, but as a continuous and interconnected communication of
God's Word to his people. This made possible an appeal to Scripture
as the final and independent criterion of doctrine, Church order and
institutions, and liturgy. That for which no warrant could be found
in Scripture was not to be demanded as essential to the Church's
teaching or to its way of life.

(a) These Anglican documents are, first, the question put by the
bishop to every candidate for the priesthood: "Are you persuaded
that the Holy Scriptures contain sufficiently all doctrine required of
necessity for eternal salvation through faith in Jesus Christ? and
are you determined, out of the said Scriptures to instruct the people
committed to your charge, and to teach nothing, as required of
necessity to eternal salvation, but that which you shall be persuaded
may be concluded and proved by the Scripture?"

(b) Secondly, several of the Articles embody the same teaching.

3

Article VI maintains the principle of *sola scriptura*, in the sense that nothing may be enjoined upon the faithful as an essential article of belief unless it can be shown to rest upon scriptural authority. "Holy Scripture containeth all things necessary to salvation : so that whatsoever is not read therein, nor may be proved thereby, is not to be required of any man, that it should be believed as an article of the Faith, or be thought requisite or necessary to salvation. . . ."

Difficult problems are presented by the expression : "whatsoever is not read therein, nor may be proved thereby". For the moment, however, I wish to go on to call attention to those other Articles which deal with the rôle of Tradition in the Church, as this was conceived of by the Anglican Reformers.

Article VIII grounds the Creeds firmly upon Scripture : "The Three Creeds . . . ought thoroughly to be received and believed : for they may be proved by most certain warrants of Holy Scripture." Thus the Creeds depend for their authority upon the fact that, as Cyril of Jerusalem had explained to his catechumens, their several clauses can be verified by anyone who takes the trouble to check them by reference to the Bible (although this criterion would be distinctly difficult to apply directly to "Athanasius' Creed", with which St Cyril was not concerned). Just as the Creeds have no authority independently of the scriptural truths which they em- body, so the enactments of General Councils are to be received in so far, and only in so far, as these are derived from Scripture.

Article XXI declares that "General Councils . . . may err, and sometimes have erred, even in things pertaining unto God. Where- fore things ordained by them as necessary to salvation have neither strength nor authority, unless it may be declared that they be taken out of Holy Scripture."

Again, to pass over for the moment the question of what is precisely meant by "taking" the things ordained by Councils "out of" Holy Scripture, let us glance at the more positive statements made by the Articles concerning Tradition.

Article XX claims authority for the Church to order its ways of worship, but not, in so doing, to contradict the written Word of God. The Church's duty is to safeguard the Scriptures, and it must neither propound anything contrary to them, nor impose any beliefs which they do not contain. "The Church hath power to decree Rites or Ceremonies, and authority in Controversies of Faith: And yet it is not lawful for the Church to ordain any thing that is contrary to God's Word written, neither may it so expound one place of Scripture, that it be repugnant to another. Wherefore, although the Church be a witness and keeper of Holy Writ, yet, as it ought not to decree any thing against the same, so besides the same ought it not to enforce any thing to be believed for necessity of Salvation."

What the sphere of the Church's independent authority includes is more clearly stated in Article XXXIV, where Traditions and Ceremonies are linked together. These, the Article says, need not be uniform throughout the Church. "At all times they have been divers, and may be changed according to the Diversities of countries, times, and men's manners, so that [provided that] nothing be ordained against God's Word." To break the traditions and ceremonies of the Church which are not repugnant to the Word of God and which are ordained and approved by common authority, through the exercise of private judgement, is an offence against the common order of the Church and against the authority of the civil power. It also wounds the consciences of the weak brethren. "Every particular or national Church hath authority to ordain, change, and abolish, ceremonies or rites of the Church ordained only by man's authority, so that all things be done to edifying."

This Article, too, raises numerous questions. It does not tell us exactly what is comprised under the heading of "Traditions". The fact that they are so closely associated with ceremonies indicates that, as in the patristic period, and indeed throughout Church history, they include the way in which things are done in the Church, and especially its forms of worship. It is more doubtful whether they also include the forms of Church order itself.

The Preface to the Ordinal appeals to "Holy Scripture and ancient authors" as evidence for its assertion that the three-fold Ministry of bishops, priests, and deacons has existed in the Church from the Apostles' time. This would suggest that this is excluded from those traditions which may vary from country to country and from time to time, and that it is a matter of divine ordinance. On the other hand it is clear that Whitgift and Hooker regarded the episcopal pattern of Church government as something sanctioned by antiquity, fully compatible with Scripture, and determined, for this country, by lawful authority; but they did not claim divine institution for it, and, as the attitude of sixteenth and much seventeenth-century Anglicanism to foreign Protestant Churches makes clear, the historic ministry was regarded as one of those traditions which a particular or national Church may change or abolish, but which the Church of England intended to retain, and which it was not open to anyone's private judgement to impugn, though, in the last resort, it was a thing indifferent. It is one of the rather ironical facts of history that in the sixteenth century it was the Presbyterian Puritans who claimed that Order was a part of Faith, and that the New Testament offered a blueprint for the future government of the Church for all time, designed by the Lord and his Apostles. The official policy of the Church of England's leaders was to deny this and to maintain that in the last resort any particular form of Church order was a thing indifferent, resting at best on godly tradition rather than on any express injunctions of Scripture. The Tractarians and their successors reversed the Anglican rôle in the dispute. It now became the Anglicans who claimed that one specific form of ministerial order was laid down in Scripture, and their opponents who regarded it as an *adiaphoron*, with the important difference that the scriptural order was now said to be episcopalian and not presbyterian. To-day the official Anglican position appears to be both that one particular form of Ministry is divinely ordained and that there is no clear scriptural evidence for this; so that an absolute requirement is based on the same sort of unwritten tradition as that on which the papal claims rest.

Article XXXIV also raises a far-reaching matter of principle which was of great importance in the controversies of the sixteenth and early seventeenth centuries. It maintains that traditions should be respected, and certainly not broken by individual action, unless they are clearly contrary to Scripture. Scripture affords a negative criterion only. It is not necessary that all traditions and ceremonies should be positively sanctioned by Scripture. In this respect the Article expresses the consistent view of the Anglican leaders against the more zealous reformers of the Geneva style. Cranmer had himself complained about those who claimed that what is not positively commanded in the Scriptures is unlawful: the great example of this being the practice of kneeling at Communion. To this Cranmer replied that if this contention were accepted one might as well abolish the service-book altogether, and indeed Church order itself: "If kneeling be not expressly enjoined in Holy Scripture, neither is standing or sitting. Let them lie down on the ground and eat their meals like Turks or Tartars." For Whitgift and Hooker the principle that what is not laid down in Scripture is unlawful was not only impossible to apply in practice, but also involved an extension of the sphere of scriptural authority into areas which were properly intended by God to fall within the scope of tradition and ordinary human reason. Scripture was meant to prescribe what is essential for salvation. Its authority concerns the ground and the content of the faith by which men are saved. On these essential matters it declares God's Word. But it was not intended as a detailed text-book of Church order, government, discipline, or modes of worship. It was not meant to be taken as a book of rules for the minutiae of daily life. These belonged properly to tradition and reason, or rather to men's reason guided by the traditions of the past, and Scripture was likely only to suffer discredit in respect of its rightful authority if it were misapplied in this fashion.

In this way the respective spheres of Scripture and tradition were roughly marked out. In the process of doing so, and of leaving room for the free exercise of reason on the relatively minor questions of religion, the Anglican Fathers left a door open through which a way was made in the later seventeenth and the eighteenth century for the exaltation of reason as the ultimate authority, and, however optimistically it might be claimed that reason and Scripture were thoroughly consonant with one another, as the criterion by which Scripture itself could be judged.

All the Anglican Reformers, nevertheless, assumed the supreme authority of Scripture. Their main difficulty naturally arose out of the problem of the Canon. It is the canonical books which are declared to be sufficient as the source and norm of saving truth. Having defined the Canon strictly, and excluded the apocryphal books from contributing to the establishment of doctrine, they were faced with the difficulty that the formation of the Canon could easily suggest that here at this point, at any rate, the authority of the Church was supreme and had in a sense created Scripture itself. Various answers were given to this problem. Patristic testimony to the supreme authority of Scripture played an important part here, and this included the witness of the Church to the apostolic, or near-apostolic authorship of the canonical books and their transmission from the earliest times. Burnet, after making this point and declaring that these books were received as apostolic "in the very apostolical age itself", points out that the formation of the Canon was not a process by which the Church deliberately selected certain books and pronounced them to be authoritative. It was rather that the Church acknowledged itself to be already subject to the authority of those books which had been consistently read in the congregation as apostolic works. "The Church's being called the witness of holy writ", he says, "is not to be resolved into any judgement that they pass upon it as a body of men that have authority to judge and give sentence, so that the canonicalness or the uncanonicalness of any book shall depend upon their testimony: but is resolved into this, that such succession and numbers of men, whether of the laity or clergy, have in the course of many ages had these books preserved and read among them."

More important, perhaps, was the general tendency to regard the authority of the canonical books, that is to say their character as "God's Word written", as being self-authenticating: or rather, as being authenticated to the reader by the inner testimony of the Holy Spirit who had inspired their authors. While, therefore, the Church could give its external testimony to the authenticity of the apostolic writings, the attestation of their contents as being nothing less than God's Word was an operation of the Holy Spirit illuminating the mind and conscience of the believer. This doctrine, which was, of course, common to the Reformers in general, could lead in principle to uncontrolled subjectivity. If the interpretation of Scripture were to be saved from the individual fancy of any and every reader, and indeed if the Canon itself were to be saved from being diminished or enlarged according to personal preferences, or to the inner witness of the Spirit in each man, the corporate experience of the Church, tradition in the form of standard exegesis, exposition, homiletic preaching, and liturgical usage, had to be appealed to as the criterion of scriptural interpretation.

In practice, this meant an appeal to the tradition contained in the Creeds, the Councils, and the Fathers. It was on the basis of the appeal to the "catholic Fathers and ancient bishops", or, as the preface to the Prayer Book has it, "the godly and decent order of the ancient Fathers", that the innovations of later medieval doctrine

and practice, including especially those which were of current importance in the controversy with Rome, were rejected. What was unknown, or at least not taught, in the early centuries, could not be claimed as essential to saving faith now. Nor could the individual fancies of the modern Bible-reader be allowed to prevail over the solid exegetical tradition of the ancient Church.

In setting up this standard there was, of course, no thought of asserting a dual norm of authority. Scripture was always supreme and decisive, and the authority of Creeds, Councils, and Fathers was entirely secondary to it. As a norm of interpretation, however, the appeal to the early Church was plausible. But it had some grave defects. It assumed a much greater unanimity of belief among the Fathers than in fact there ever existed. A general consensus of patristic teaching can be discovered only at the price of first establishing a narrow canon of patristic orthodoxy, such as was in fact set up by the Tractarians in selecting authors for their "Library of the Fathers", from which some distinguished names are conspicuously absent. Even then, if we are to find such a consensus we shall probably have to ignore many inconsistencies or changes of mood in individual authors. The easiest way to make the Fathers present a united front on any particular topic is to select a catena of suitable passages from their works, extracted from their proper context and arranged to give support to a preconceived point of view. By this means it is possible to get the Fathers, like the Bible itself, to support any conceivable religious opinion; and this method was in fact widely prevalent in the sixteenth century, as Cranmer's catena of citations on justification by faith alone, or the various eucharistic anthologies, clearly show. Indeed, this was a method which persisted until quite modern times.

A further defect was the difficulty of deciding how early the early Church was, or rather what were the chronological limits of the age of the "Fathers". One might speak of the "undivided Church" or of the period which saw the emergence of the creeds and the conciliar definitions; but in practice the patristic period as a standard of biblical interpretation tended to vary according to the subject under discussion. On most issues it was restricted to the first five centuries, or, as by Jewel, the first six; but in respect of eucharistic doctrine it was much more generously extended, so as to include the period of the Berengarian controversy. In other words, recourse was often had to the Fathers to justify teaching that in fact rested mainly upon contemporary thinking about the scriptural data. The patristic teaching was more often a reinforcement than a source for the Reformers' doctrine, and as such it represents an arbitrary restriction to a fixed period of history and a limited number of theologians of what should be a much wider appeal to the universal *consensus fidelium* and to the rational principle that change, renewal, and reformation in response to current thought and contemporary needs are legitimate when they constitute a development on lines suggested by the original Gospel itself.

The problem for the sixteenth century, as for all Christians, was how, on the one hand, to avoid a mere biblicism which seeks to apply the thought and practice of the first century directly and without modification to a very different contemporary situation, and, on the other hand, to find a norm for controlling the development of Christian devotion and thought, and guarding the original Gospel from serious distortion. The problem is always with us; but the solutions that were confidently proposed in the age of the Reformation are no longer possible for us to accept without drastic modification.

We are confronted, first of all, with the question of what we mean by "authority" in matters of belief. The arguments of the sixteenth century were carried on within the framework of a presupposition, shared by all parties, that salvation depended on a correct intellectual attitude towards certain propositions. For a man to be saved, as the Athanasian Creed declared, it was above all things necessary that he should hold the Catholic Faith. This Catholic Faith was a system of propositions concerning, so far as this Creed goes, the Trinity and the Person of Christ, couched in the developed forms of fifth century credal orthodoxy, but finding their authority as revealed truth in their "provability" by reference to Scripture. The questions which exercise both sides in the Reformation disputes were concerned only with the extent and number of those propositions to which assent ought rightly to be "required" of any man as articles of the Faith, or thought "requisite or necessary" to salvation: not with the prior question whether assent to any such propositions can properly be "required" or whether orthodoxy is necessary for salvation. Did these propositions

include only those which might either be read directly out of
Scripture (such as, that Jesus ascended into heaven), or be shown
to be consistent with and, indeed, implicitly contained in Scripture
although not explicitly set forth there (such as, that the Son is
consubstantial with the Father, or that deity and humanity are
hypostatically united in the one Person of Christ)? Or did they also
include propositions about which nothing is said in Scripture either
directly or indirectly (such as, that the substance of the eucharistic
bread is changed by consecration into that of the body of Christ),
but which claimed the sanction of tradition? Both parties were
committed to the idea that intellectual acceptance of some propositions is absolutely necessary for salvation. Whatever the status
of tradition-based dogmas might be, everyone was agreed that the
Scriptures formed a supreme text-book of saving divinity. The Bible
was the great source-book from which all Christians might learn
necessary articles of belief and be instructed about the kind of
conduct which assent to these dogmas ought to involve.

Professor Nineham has recently called attention to the persistence
of the idea that the Bible offers to Christians "a collection of
inerrant propositions and irreformable demands and prohibitions,
guaranteed by their direct divine origin as timelessly valid and
universally binding". He continues: "Those who, in Calvinistic
circles, for example, insisted on the literal acceptance of certain
biblical statements—those relating to the so-called 'plan of salvation'—at the expense of implicitly ignoring the rest; even those
liberal modernists who in effect anthologized the Bible, frankly
jettisoning many of its statements in the belief that the rest would
vindicate themselves as 'timeless truths' about the relations between
God and man; all these in their various ways subscribed to the sort
of view of the Bible I have been describing." Such a view of the
relation of dogmas to the Bible as their source is still widely
prevalent; but it belongs to the past. To attempt to find in
Scripture direct "proof" of what are, in fact, much later developments of Christian doctrine is an activity proper only to an age
which has not begun to think historically; and it is the historical
revolution of the past century which, far more than any other
factor, has made the view of scriptural authority which we find in
the Anglican formularies untenable.

Jowett had already seen this point when in *Essays and Reviews* he complained that it is by no means easy to say what it means to "prove" a doctrine from Scripture. To try to do so involves an attempt to bring Scripture into line with later orthodoxy. Indeed, it is hard to see how, on a pre-critical and pre-historical understanding of the meaning of scriptural proof, it is really possible to prove from the Bible a doctrine, such as the penal interpretation of Christ's death, or the full Chalcedonian understanding of his Person, without in fact making Scripture subservient to later tradition. Moreover, it presupposes, as Jowett saw clearly, that a uniform dogmatic system is to be discovered in the biblical writings themselves. "When we demand logical equivalents and similarity of circumstances," he wrote, "when we balance adverse statements, St James and St Paul, the New Testament with the Old, it will be hard to demonstrate from Scripture any complex system of doctrine or practice." As long as Scripture was in fact regarded as a source-book of dogma it was impossible to receive its witness, in and through historical situations, to God's Word addressed to man in the particularity of actual human circumstances, speaking of mercy and judgement, grace and demand, or to understand that what is requisite for salvation is response to this Word and not the acceptance of a particular system of propositions. Yet Scripture was so regarded from a very early date, one of the unfortunate consequences of this view being the adoption by the Church of the Old Testament as a text-book of Christian belief and practice, so that Hebrew legislation about sacrifice, priesthood, the sabbath (to name only a very few points out of many) gradually came to be applied directly to Christian worship, the ministry of the Church, and the observance of Sunday.

Even so, it was still not really possible to submit Christian doctrine and practice to the letter of Scripture as a purely objective criterion, for Scripture itself was not read in a spirit of scientific objectivity, but through spectacles furnished by exegetical tradition and sometimes also by the ingenuity of individual preachers and commentators. Since typological, and, often, allegorical, exegesis was required in order to elicit spiritual edification from apparently dull, unimportant, or scandalous passages, much depended on the extent and the degree of the *gnosis* which a skilled and ingenious interpreter could bring to bear on the text. In this way the subjective outlook of the exegete and the presuppositions with which he worked, whether his own or the Church's, went far to mitigate the apparent rigour of the appeal to Scripture. Indeed, they often enabled Scripture to be conformed to ecclesiastical tradition rather than the other way round; and although the Reformers deprecated allegorism and sought to follow the plain literal sense, subjective allegorism, by which developed doctrine could be read back into Scripture, continued to be widely prevalent until very recent times and is not yet dead. This is what Jowett was contending against when he urged that the Bible must be read like any other book. He meant that it must be allowed to speak for itself, and that the first duty of the interpreter is to try so far as possible to discover what the original author meant to say, and not to force the text into conformity with external dogmatic systems.

Yet it is not enough simply to insist upon this truth, fundamentally important though it is. The task of exegesis is undoubtedly to understand and expound, as closely as may be, what the biblical authors were saying, in the language and forms of thought of their own time, to their contemporaries. If the exegete tries to go beyond this duty he ceases to do exegesis. But when he has done his exegesis the Christian interpreter is faced with the task of relating the conclusions of exegesis to the on-going life, thought, and worship of the Christian Society. For the Church encounters Jesus Christ not simply as an historical character in the pages of an ancient book, but as its living Lord who becomes contemporary with itself through the continuing witness of the Holy Spirit in the corporate and individual life of its members, more especially through preaching and the sacraments. Christ is always at the same time past, present, and future to his people. The Lord whose gracious presence is mediated now by the Spirit in the community is the same who was once, in the past, present as the individual physical entity of the carpenter of Nazareth. The Lord who was present as the historical figure who was crucified is the one to whose glorified likeness the people of God hope to be conformed at the end, in the age of fulfilment. To write about the historical Jesus is, or ought to be, impossible for a Christian without seeking to relate him to, or rather to identify him with, the present Lord of the Church and the object of its future hope. To speak of the Lord who through the Spirit creates the society of his people to be his Body is, or should be, impossible without identifying him with the man who was

crucified. Nevertheless, to hold history and present experience together is no easy task, and the tension which it creates has existed
since before the extreme positions of Ebionites and Gnostics were
marked out in the second century. For it is this inevitable tension
which sets us the problem of Scripture and Tradition and the
authority which should belong to each.

In one sense Scripture represents the historical given-ness of the
revelation in Christ. It witnesses to the event itself, in the context of
God's ancient revelation to Israel. In Christ God has acted
decisively within human history. Scripture contains the record of
the works and words of Jesus in and through which the divine
action was effected. It might seem at first sight that Scripture could
be said to correspond to the "finished work" of Christ, and that
Scripture is "sufficient" because the work of God in Christ is
sufficient for man's salvation. It might further seem that tradition
could be said to correspond to the continuing application of Christ's
once-for-all completed work to men as they receive it by faith
and appropriate its benefits. Scripture would thus embody the
given-ness of revelation; tradition its subjective apprehension.

But this would be to over-simplify the matter. If by "tradition"
we may mean the on-going experience of the Church, appropriated
and developed by successive generations, then we have to admit at
the outset that Scripture itself is written out of that experience,
and is therefore itself a part of the tradition. Tradition and Scripture
cannot rightly be set over against each other as though they represent two quite different modes of God's self-disclosure. For us who
live in the age of form-criticism it is obviously unthinkable to do
this. The Gospels represent the mind of those who stood within the
Church's tradition; those who shared its Easter faith and lived in
the consciousness of the Lordship of the risen Christ. They are
written from the standpoint of men who had received the tradition
(that is, the continuing experience of the living Lord through, or as,
the Holy Spirit in the community), as this experience had been
transmitted by the preaching, teaching, and general "contagion"
of those whose lives were already governed and motivated by that
experience.

The Gospels, in any case, are but a part of the New Testament
Scriptures. The Epistles clearly stand in the context of the Church's
life as it was lived in the light of the Resurrection. They are a part

of the tradition, reflecting the experience of the community, and especially its leaders, as they work out the meaning and the practical implications of their conviction that Jesus is Lord. This experience, the tradition of the post-Easter community, is reflected back into that part of Scripture, the Gospels, which seems at first sight to present us with the objective historical given-ness of the work and words of Jesus. These Gospels are concerned to show that the one who walked in Galilee and was of the race of David was none other than the one whom the Church now knew as its Lord, who had been defined as Son of God through the Resurrection. They witness to the earthly figure as being the Lord of all.

Hence in the Gospels the past is interpreted in the light of the present. The living tradition of the Church's worship, catechizing, preaching, and other activities is the source of the evangelists' material. Paul reminds his Corinthian readers of the teaching about the Lord's Supper which had been committed to him and which he had in turn transmitted to them. This was something which belonged to the continuing tradition of the risen Christ's people before it was ever written down as part of the scriptural record of the historical Jesus. Sometimes the present faith of the community projects its beliefs about the Lordship of Jesus and its implications in the concrete form of stories about the past which these beliefs actually create. So I should interpret, among other narratives, those of the infancy. They express in concrete form the belief that in Jesus the expectations of the prophets of Israel have been fulfilled and in the story of the virgin birth, the conviction of those who now believed in Jesus' Lordship that in his earthly life he was one who was a human being and yet also one who came from God : one whose life was in one sense continuous with that of all man-kind before him, and yet in another sense was so wholly new as to be God's fresh creation, breaking the line of descent from Adam and bringing in God's new humanity. Here tradition, in the sense of the Church's continuing and developing experience of faith, has created Scripture out of its own insights. I think that the same applies to the stories of the empty tomb, among others. Where tradition has not created, it has selected, modified, applied in new ways, and generally moulded the original historical data, that is to say the testimony of eyewitnesses. Scripture thus presents us with the witness of the Church to its Lord, expressed, in certain parts of the New Testament, in the form of a history of the past. Scripture therefore *is* tradition.

Yet while the New Testament writers were thus concerned to reinterpret the historical Jesus as the Lord of the Church's post-Resurrection faith, they were also insistent that the Church's Lord was none other than the historical Jesus. He whom God had made Lord and Christ was none other than the Jesus who had been crucified. This is the constant theme of the early preaching. It is the reason why so much of the Church's faith came to be embodied in the peculiar form of "gospels", stories about Jesus in the pre-Easter situation. Those who lived in the tradition, sharing in the developing experience of Christ as the Lord of glory, could never forget that this tradition, this continuing experience, was firmly rooted in certain historical events. That existential situation of Christian believers was directly related to a particular individual man, Jesus of Nazareth. Christian faith remains bound to that history and cannot be dissolved into any form of timeless *gnosis* without destroying its essential nature. The continuing tradition of the Lord's Supper, and the experience of the Lord's active presence among his people of which it was the focus, a present anticipation of the Parousia, were read back into the pre-Easter situation and no doubt determined much of the content and character of the Gospel narratives of the Last Supper, the miraculous feedings, and the Resurrection appearances. But this tradition was itself *received* tradition. It is most improbable that there would have been any tradition in this case without an historical event or events to give rise to it. However many question-marks may have to be placed against particular episodes and against the details of narratives, the Gospels embody not only the developing faith of the post-Resurrection Church but also, in the last resort, the testimony of those who were eyewitnesses and ministers of the Word.

The tradition of the primitive Church, interpreting the past in the light of present experience, and at the same time linking present experience firmly to a past event, is uniquely important. It is a part of the continuous stream of tradition in the Church, but it is constitutive and regulative of all that follows it. This is partly due to chronology. It stands relatively close to the original events, and, at however distant a remove, it embodies and depends upon an original core of eyewitness record. When we have again made all allowances for the question-marks that may be set against specific items in the material, it is obviously true that it is upon these documents that we depend for virtually all our information about Jesus as an historical figure, and about the rise and growth of the Christian Church. This is not the factor, however, that is most important in making this part of the tradition normative. It is by no means certain that a direct record by eyewitnesses of the acts and sayings of Jesus would be as valuable as the witness of Paul, Mark, or the Fourth Evangelist. Indeed, for his part, the Fourth Evangelist quite evidently thought not. The things concerning Jesus could not be properly understood or "remembered" until, after his glorification, the Spirit could interpret him in the light of the Resurrection.

The importance of this first part of the tradition lies in the fact that the writers who have preserved it are witnesses to the two-fold impact of Jesus Christ, the historical figure and the risen Lord. They present to us the experience of those who first came to faith in one whom they remembered, or of whom they knew, as the man who was crucified, and whom they had also encountered through, or as, the Spirit in the community of believers. They are witnesses to the earthly and to the exalted Christ, for even if they did not see the earthly Christ in the flesh they stood near enough to those who had done so. Hence the tradition which they formed, handed on, and embodied in what became the canonical writings, is normative for all the rest; for subsequent tradition cannot create gospels, but is rather the explication of this primary witness through dogmatic formulation and above all through the process of working out in thought and life what is involved in it. This in part explains why neither the apostles nor the evangelists have successors. Their function as primary witnesses, standing at the point where memory of the events combines with faith in the exalted Lord, is not transmissible. Hence this first part of the Church's tradition came inevitably to be acknowledged as the norm and canonized as Scripture, while all that follows is commentary and unfolding.

This function of subsequent tradition gives rise to what may be called a double process of checking. The Lord is not a mere "founder of Christianity" with whom we are linked only by historical records or institutional continuity. He is the living and contemporary Lord, made present through the Spirit. Hence, on the one hand, the witness of the earliest believers, and their successors down the centuries, can be checked and verified at every step by the criterion of the Church's present experience. We can properly ask, in Dr Hodgson's words, "What must the truth have been if it appeared like this to men who thought and spoke like that?" We can go further and ask whether what the earliest believers thought is right for us to believe in the light of our experience : to ask, that is to say, whether the Bible is right for us. Thus, for instance, we may ask whether the New Testament says enough, or says the right things, about Christian marriage, or the Christian's duty to the State, or how Christ's death is the means of reconciling us to God. But if Scripture itself may be checked against the present experience of the Church collectively and of its individual members, it remains true that this present experience, if it is of any value, will itself have been conditioned by, and derived from, reflection on the earliest part of the tradition (that is, Scripture) in the light of new insights and changing circumstances. What St Paul said about marriage can be judged by us : but we shall judge it by the general purport or tendency of the Scriptures as this is seen and understood in the light of the guidance of the Spirit, communicated to us through the thought and experience of mankind both inside and outside the Church. For if the earliest tradition may be checked by present experience, it is even more necessary that present experience should be checked against, and judged by the scriptural witness. If this is not done, present experience tends to fashion Scripture after its own likeness and to reduce the earliest testimony until it fits conveniently into such categories as those of the "liberal Jesus", *Heilsgeschichte*, or the "biblical drama" which made so strong an appeal to the last Lambeth Conference. Indeed, it is only in this way that present experience can be sure of remaining *Christian* experience, related to a Lord who is still identical with the historical figure. Present experience will not convey God's Word to us unless it is constantly subjected to the judgement of God's incarnate Word speaking, whether at first or second hand, through those who knew him in both his lowliness and his glory.

In the last resort, the ultimate authority for us is our present and personal experience of Jesus Christ as Lord, and the total commitment which this entails. This is the faith for which martyrs die. It carries an absolute authority. Such experience is created in us, or, as we may equally express it, faith is evoked in us, by the experience of his original followers as that has been communicated to us through their writings and through the preaching, and the interpretation in word and action of others who have themselves shared in it. The experience of these others has sometimes modified the original witness, reformulated it, and interpreted it in new ways; but in its essentials it is controlled by the original witness. This original witness, which we call Scripture, explicated by, sometimes reinterpreted by, but always ultimately controlling and judging the subsequent tradition, evokes faith. Hence it is authoritative in so far as it evokes that commitment and obligation to obedience which is the ultimate authority for us: that is, in so far as the Spirit makes it a channel of God's Word.

The subsequent tradition is secondary, being interpretative and explanatory rather than creative. Credal and other doctrinal formulations are highly important and weighty statements of the ways in which the Church, in the light of its developing experience, has endeavoured to understand and explain the meaning of its primary commitment to Christ as Lord. In so far as they continue to help believers to do this they are authoritative, somewhat in the manner in which the past findings of experts in any particular branch of study are authoritative. It is not an absolute authority, however, and if at any time such formulations, despite their scriptural basis, cease to prove illuminating, they have then lost their authority, at least for the time being, and may need to be revised or discarded.

DISCUSSION

DR MARTIN SCHMIDT opened discussion on Canon Lampe's paper. He said:

Since I agree essentially with the basic tendency of what we have just heard, I should like to develop some of the thoughts and give them a sharper edge to start discussion.

The result of Canon Lampe's excellent study — so very meticulous in the pursuit of evidence, so wide in its scope and balanced in its judgement — seems to be the invalidation of the alternative between Scripture and Tradition as the basis of ecclesiastical authority and ecclesiastical standards. Rather, it establishes that all claims to authority in the history of Christianity bear the character of Tradition, with the result that the task now is to make a well-founded choice between various traditions. The question for every Christian generation is this: What is the "best" Tradition? This must not be understood in the historical sense of a documentary dependence upon proximity to events that can be proved, but in the sense of its content as conveying a genuine nearness to the impression left upon the disciples by the person and work of Jesus. This nearness of impression can be apprehended only through what the believer as an individual and the Church as the fellowship of believers has experienced and continues to experience. Such experience gives rise to a deep and direct mutual sharing which continues through changing times. This agreement, as far as it can be expressed in words — though there is no need to pursue it to the point of agreement in precise formulas — is the central presupposition behind the formation of the Canon.

Scripture, as Canon, is not revelation in the direct sense but witness to revelation, that is, a product of those men who were best able to vouch for the content of the event of divine self-disclosure which took place in the person and work of Jesus Christ. This concept of Lampe's approximates most closely in German Evangelical theology to that of Wilhelm Herrmann and its further development by Gerhard Ebeling.

The claim of the Canon to be regulative — regulative as distinct from normative — rests on the superiority of what is original over what is derived, and on the greater weight attaching to a common experience of faith as compared with individual experience. Not only has the Canon the right to correct the latter; rather it unlocks the very person of Jesus for all who come after him and it makes him accessible. For that reason it is irreplaceable. Significantly enough, it exists in a double form: first, as the Word of proclamation which called the Church into being as the successor of Jesus; and then, as the handing on of this Word and its history as it was established by the Church. Thus the Canon is both the point of departure for the Church and also a process of expansion in the Church, primary as well as secondary in relation to her, a fixed point as well as a flexible movement.

If, in the wake of the historical-critical studies of the Bible in the last two and a half centuries, we were to attempt to dissolve the Canon into its various parts and lay bare the currents of tradition behind them; and if we were to let the contemporary Christian freely choose between, say, a tradition according to the primitive Church, or a Pauline, Lucan, or Johannine tradition, or a (limited) recognition of the Old Testament—depending on his spiritual attitude to one or other of these various traditions—we should be disregarding the common experience of believers, as was done in Germany with particularly long-lasting effect by Johann Gottlieb Fichte. Fichte rejected the Pauline concept of justification in favour of the Johannine mysticism of love; he also rejected the concept of creation in favour of a metaphysic of being. What is more, we should fail to understand the situation of the first witnesses, of whom it is characteristic that their experience of faith was reflected in such a wide variety of statements. Dogmatically speaking, we should be disobeying the will of God, for he has allotted to men this diversity as a continuous situation and the struggle between orthodoxy and heresy as a continuous task.

What are the consequences of the view expressed?

1. The concept of "Scripture" becomes flexible. It is understood neither as a dogmatic arsenal of inerrant and absolutely valid statements all on the same level, nor as the infallible product of an untouchable sacred history. Rather it enters within the lowliness of all history, within concrete historicity with all its uncertainties, its "chances", and its dependence on subjective accounts and prejudices. Scripture is history in its fullest sense.

Dogmatically speaking, it makes evident the data of the Incarnation of God, his subjection to the form of a servant under earthly conditions, his surrender to the human limitations of error, arbitrariness, and incapacity.

Whenever Scripture is used as a means of proof in Christian argumentation, it really has to be worked upon. It is not sufficient simply to refer to it. The history to which Scripture testifies must be co-ordinated with the contemporary Christian's own experience of history.

2. The concept of "authority" becomes flexible. Authority is in accordance with the first Christians' experience of faith — an accordance freely accepted because it is based on conviction. Authority is the humble acceptance of the fact of the Incarnation as handed down and given to us — the Incarnation of divine revelation within history (to which both Old and New Testaments bear witness).

The fact that the phenomenon "authority" (ἐξουσία, δύναμις) is shown in the New Testament itself in such great variety corresponds with this concept. R. R. Williams in particular [1] has pointed to such a variety: in the narratives of events, miracles, encounters; in exhortations, dominical words, counsels, ministries, rites. In considering the context of each we always have to ask whether it is the ultimate authority of God in Jesus Christ which is disclosed or the penultimate authority of his disciples.

3. If "Scripture" becomes "Tradition", then tradition too loses its distinctive position both as the key to Scripture and as the continuation of revelation. The Roman Catholic definition of their mutual relation is thus no longer possible.

With reference to the historical *excursus* on the problem of Scripture and Tradition in Anglican theology, which is a particular interest of mine and therefore of great value to me, I venture to put the following question:

Is it not true that both John Whitgift and Richard Hooker recognized in tradition (that is, post-biblical tradition) and in the legal order of England a basis for the episcopal office; but that

---

[1] *Authority in the Apostolic Age*, 1950.

already Lancelot Andrews,[2] through his christological derivation
of the Church's ministries, ascribed to the episcopal office a biblical
—that is, a divine—right? This would mean that the Puritans of the
Calvinist type were not the sole champions of the "jus divinum"
in those early days.

FURTHER DISCUSSION touched first upon the content of
"saving faith". This, it was said, must always have its basis in
certain historical facts enshrined in the Gospel. The Incarnation not
only demonstrated that God was in the midst of men in a universal
sense; the events of the Incarnation were contingent within history,
and those events were the content of the witness forming the
original tradition. The Augsburg Confession (*Confessio Augustana* I
i) lays a great emphasis upon the content of what is to be believed
("credendum esse").[3] All agreed, however, that there were two
levels of belief: belief in certain statements about Christ and belief
in Christ himself. We are saved by Christ, not by any philosophy
about him. To set "fides quae creditur" over against "fides qua
creditur" was therefore to pose a false alternative. These two may
be distinguishable but they are quite inseparable. Furthermore,
saving faith involves not only belief in God but sanctification—an
emphasis much stressed by the Eastern Orthodox tradition.

Tribute was paid to Professor Lampe's carefully balanced statement about the relation between Scripture and Tradition. Some
participants, especially on the German side, were somewhat
hesitant to embody Scripture totally within Tradition. It was asked
whether, on this view, Scripture could still be said to exercise any
control over Tradition. Was an historical judgement about the
origin of the New Testament being confused with a theological
judgement? It was generally agreed that the true distinction had
been most clearly formulated when described as a distinction
between "original tradition" and "derived tradition".

This raised the question of a criterion for determining what was
original and what was derived. Was there any standard by which to

2 "A summary View of the Government both of the Old and New
Testament" in *Minor Works* (Libr. of Anglo-Catholic Theology), 1846, pp.
337-62.

3 Cf. Ehlert, *Morphologie des Luthertums*.

measure the central core of the scriptural message—that is, to discover an inner unity lying behind the diversity of traditions evident even within Scripture. This raised the problem of the *Eindeutigkeit* of Scripture. A German delegate reminded the Conference that Luther in his critical approach to the Canon distinguished between "claritas externa" and "claritas interna", which may correspond to the distinction made earlier in discussion between an historical judgement and a theological judgement, or between original tradition and derived tradition. Luther was no biblicist: his primary appeal was to the *doctrina evangelica* and his appeal to Scripture was secondary. He pointed to the Gospel of Jesus Christ (*das Evangelium*) as being the central core of Scripture. The Gospel itself, in this sense, is the living centre not only of Scripture but of all credal statements.

In conclusion, it was agreed that, although to say "Scripture is Tradition" may be helpful in avoiding the impasse of Reformation squabbles, we must maintain that the New Testament, as Scripture, belongs to a definite category of material, αἱ γραφαί, in common with the Old Testament, which is not merely μαρτυρία. It is the essential content of Scripture, the Gospel of Jesus Christ, which distinguishes it conclusively from all the products of Greek philosophy.

AFTERNOON DISCUSSION was opened by Canon H. E. W. Turner. He said:

All would agree that the ultimate starting point for thinking about Authority must be the authority of Christ himself in his Totality— Incarnate, Crucified, Risen, Ascended, Glorified—both in his "once-for-allness" (*Einmaligkeit*) and in his ongoing life in the Church.

To this polarity in our understanding of Christ, the relation between Scripture and Tradition appears to correspond. There is a "once-for-allness" about Scripture which makes the relation between Scripture and Tradition theologically as well as historically irreversible. The two are related as the Given and the Derived or (to use Lutheran language) as the *norma normans* and the *norma normata*. The primacy of Scripture would be accepted by all Christians. Yet tradition (though derivative and dependent upon

30335

Scripture) is inevitable and does not lack its own (though secondary) authority.

1. *The Primacy of Scripture*

Against the view outlined above two objections might be raised.

(*a*) It is argued that historically Scripture forms part of Tradition. This historical judgement does not, however, demand a similar answer to the dogmatic question. For Scripture, in so far as it was current and received at any given time, was always the normative part of the Tradition. Nor is this view excluded by the wide range of early interpretations of Christianity to which Walter Bauer called attention. There certainly existed in the second century a wide penumbra of views between which selection was only gradually made. A problem has also been found in the growth of the New Testament Canon. While its completion for all parts of the Church does not antedate the fifth century, considerable progress was already made by the end of the second century. The question whether the Church created or recognized the Canon of Scripture conceals an important ambiguity. Historically no doubt the Church *created* the Canon in the sense of determining its limits; in a theological and far more important sense, it *recognized* Scripture by acknowledging the normative character for faith and life of this particular corpus of writings.

(*b*) The diversity of Scripture has also been taken as an objection to this view. This is no new problem (it is already recognized in Luther's treatment of the New Testament) but it has been given a new actuality through the application of historical and critical techniques to the Bible. Many employ a kind of "Canon within the Canon" or italicize one key-feature as a norm or centre of reference. We may perhaps compare the dictum of St Athanasius that the "σκοπός of Scripture is itself Scripture". Either or both techniques are legitimate and neither incompatible with the view here proposed. We can speak of the New Testament on its more human side at least as a convergence of testimony to Christ. New Testament diversity is comparable to a symphony which can include discords within it rather than to a single melodic theme, or even to a set of very similar variations.

Scripture then has the Primacy, and represents the given norm from which Tradition is derived and to which it must always be related. This order is theologically as well as historically irreversible.

2. *The Inevitability of Tradition*

Tradition, however, is not only legitimate but also inevitable. A recent description of Tradition as "the worldliness of the Church" does much less than justice to its rightful place. No doubt in certain cases traditions can be described as worldly or Tradition itself interpreted or used in ways which might merit this description. But so long as it is held in proper relation of derivation from and dependence upon Scripture it remains a norm, a subordinate standard of reference.

Tradition is a term which can be used in a number of different senses. There is tradition in ethos, which has an obvious bearing upon tradition in doctrine though it is hardly identical with it. There is tradition displayed in customs and usages (what to-day would be described as "traditions" and normally taken as standing on a lower level theologically than the other sense). Tradition can also be expressed in organization, the necessary scaffolding of a corporate Christian existence. Here the Ministry and its forms stand on a higher level than offices like archdeacons, rural deans, and canons, in and out of residence. There is tradition in liturgy, which is certainly not doctrinally insignificant. But it is the sense of tradition in doctrine with which we are primarily concerned here.

Here two points appear to arise which are related but not identical: control and cross-fertilization.

(a) Control. Clearly not every doctrinal development which falls within the scope of Tradition is legitimate. From the point of view of its biblical starting-point both Arius and St Athanasius represented developments, but only the latter commended himself to the Church as acceptable. Some developments may be regarded as legitimate expansions of Scripture, as integrations of the biblical subject-matter or as the conceptual framework necessary to support the primary Christian affirmation (for example, the Nicene or Chalcedonian formulations). But it is also necessary to recognize the tendency of Tradition to produce developments solely in the interests of a more complete and rounded theological system, often

to the point of losing biblical dynamism or even of obscuring or contradicting important biblical insights and principles. Recent Mariological definitions may be taken as an example on both counts. The necessity for devising criteria to distinguish these two types of development was recognized by Cardinal Newman in his famous Essay on Development. I should wish to go further and speak of the control of Tradition by Scripture.

(*b*) *Cross-fertilization*. This is a problem basically of *Sitz im Leben*. For Tradition is not merely concerned to think together the biblical data, but also to relate them to the contemporary intellectual and spiritual setting.

(i) The classical period of the development of Christian doctrine took place at a time in which the Church had moved from its original Hebraic setting into the Hellenistic world. The attempt to express the biblical data in Greek thought-forms was not, as Harnack supposed, a mark of the faithlessness but of the faithfulness of the Church. The attempt to relate Christianity to a new *Sitz im Leben* was an experiment in cross-fertilization. The result inevitably led to elements both of loss and gain, for translation into a different conceptual language can produce under- or over-translation as well as exact linguistic and conceptual equivalence. But the Creeds as crystallizations of this enterprise remain a *norma normata* in the sense that no man can call himself an orthodox Christian to-day who would not at this period have produced or accepted these conclusions.

(ii) The Reformation which produced our subordinate standards of faith represented a different *Sitz im Leben*. Its motive force consisted of the rediscovery with compelling force of biblical insights which had become obscured or distorted by much medieval religion. Many of these insights were won for all time, but some Anglicans to-day would claim that the way in which they were expressed in our subordinate standards no longer has theological currency to-day. Yet it can be maintained that no man ought to call himself an Anglican to-day who would not have reached these particular conclusions in the conditions of the sixteenth century. Many Anglicans in fact even to-day are more tenaciously retentive of the content of the Articles than this dictum would suggest.

(iii) To-day the task of restating the biblical data and the

Historical Faith in new categories remains an urgent and even an overdue task. The conceptual framework of the patristic age and even the thought-forms of the Reformation period are no longer exchangeable intellectual currency. But any attempted reformulation of the Christian Faith must have two objectives. It must be faithful to the biblical data, otherwise it becomes "another Gospel"; and it must retain the balances and emphases of the Historic Faith, otherwise it surrenders positions which have been in principle won for all time. In this task of difficulty and opportunity we are moving into the unknown and seemingly hostile territory, though we have the achievements and warnings of the past to guide us. We have not passed this way before, but others before us have made similar journeys into the unknown.

This statement of the relation between Scripture and Tradition as authorities for doctrine leaves some important questions unanswered.

(*a*) *The place of Reason in Christian theology*. No one would deny the place of reasoning in theology, but some would regard Reason as a third voice interrupting or co-operating in the dialogue between Scripture and Tradition. This seems to be involved in the analysis of Tradition which we have offered above, particularly in the recognition of changes in *Sitz im Leben* and the measures required to meet them. It is certainly demanded when what are virtually new problems arise which cannot be answered directly from the Bible or by an appeal to Tradition. A comparable situation arose in the third century when the appeal to the past represented by the arguments from apostolic tradition and succession had to be supplemented by the developing machinery of synods which could determine the mind of the Church on new problems as they arose. Perhaps in their assessment of the place of reason in theology, a difference in theological texture between the Anglican and Lutheran traditions begins to emerge.

(*b*) Old problems may be seen in new perspectives. This may extend even to the practical applications of Scripture (for example the position of women in the Church and the Christian attitude to the State). With Tradition this may be carried further. It is the balance of a doctrine, the "proportion of faith" and not the terminology in which it is expressed which represents the secondary doctrinal norm.

(*c*) New problems may arise where Scripture can give only the basic insights, and to which Tradition does not provide the key. Thus the expression of the Christian doctrine of Creation in an age of science involves a complete re-thinking of the style or idiom of the Will of God in the created order. It is not that God permits himself to be divested of his dominion under the pressure of the evolutionary theory, but that the biblical dynamism of Creation must seek expression in new ways and under new forms. Again, we cannot meet the challenge of the New Humanism merely by repeating the doctrine of St Augustine or of Calvin. What has been called the Humanist Frame is too widely removed from that of previous classical answers to permit them to be immediately relevant. Doubtless the same biblical word must be spoken to the twentieth-century humanist as to men of all ages, but he is not likely to listen or to be able to hear unless the theologian is capable first of entering into his situation, of understanding the new elements in his framework and of translating this biblical word into terms which are within earshot of our contemporaries.

FOLLOWING Canon Turner's remarks it was observed that both biblical language and credal statements were inadequate as idioms in which to convey the Gospel to the modern *Sitz im Leben*. Classical questions of faith and practice are inevitably being raised in totally new perspectives, and this inevitably involves the rôle of Reason alongside of Tradition and Scripture. An English delegate suggested that the concept of the Mind of Christ may help to serve as a criterion of the inner Canon of scripture. It also offered a more illuminating approach to the discussion of authority in the realm of Christian ethics. It is an over-simplification to ask, "What would Christ have done?" in modern and unprecedented situations. The Christian man in the modern situation must allow his mind to be apprehended by the Mind of Christ, and permit the Holy Spirit to guide his ethical decision in the present. St Paul's phrase in 1 Corinthians 3, "We have the mind of Christ", implies that the νοῦς of man has been apprehended by Christ. The Holy Spirit brings to our remembrance what Christ said; he takes the things of Christ and declares them to us (John 14. 16).

Closer attention was also given to the sense in which Tradition is sometimes referred to as the worldliness of the Church. It should be recognized that within the Church there has always been a tradition of anti-Christ (cf. the Jacob-Esau conflict in the old Israel). The worldliness of the Church is an ever-present factor in the handing on of the Gospel. St Paul pointed out the danger of the "letter" or "written code" which kills, as contrasted with the Spirit which gives life (2 Cor. 3). However, when we speak of an inner and central tradition lying behind the diverse traditions evident in Scripture, implying by this what Lutheran terminology means by "the Gospel", tradition is being seen as a work of the Spirit. Precision is therefore necessary in the use of the term "Tradition" to make clear whether it is being used in the sense of the worldliness of the Church or in the sense of the Spirit's continuous activity within the community of believers.

All agreed that since the centre of the κήρυγμα was Christ himself, there could be no question of shifting the centre of emphasis from him in understanding Scripture. The κήρυγμα points to Christ himself and requires man's decision: "What think ye of Christ?"

IN DRAWING together discussion at the end of the day, it was generally agreed that Scripture and Tradition stood in a mutual relationship which could not be reversed. This question had its beginnings in the New Testament itself: there stood the figure of Jesus of Nazareth, yet no objective account of him was available since the Event was wrapped up in the faith of the original witnesses. However, the witness was not identical with the Event.

The relationship between the Event and the witness to it is the same as that between God's demand and man's response: God addresses men in the person of Jesus, and man's response is to confess Jesus as Lord.

We as believing Christians swim, as it were, in a stream of Scripture and Tradition which flows from a single source, Jesus Christ, towards a single goal, the ἔσχατον. The eschatological aspect of the *ordo salutis* should not be lost from view.

One German participant saw in the prologue to St Luke's Gospel an indication of the unrest within the early Christian community, and went on to show that within the New Testament period

Tradition was used as an argument against outbursts of enthusiasm. 1 Corinthians 7–15 illustrated well this polemical function of Tradition, and so did the existence of hymnological material within the Epistles; the formation of the Gospels could be regarded in a similar light.

In summarizing the essential content of the Gospel lying at the heart of all Tradition, it was asked how Christ could be distinguished from all other religious figures and teachers of righteousness, be they Jewish, Hellenistic, or otherwise. A German delegate said that the distinguishing criterion about Christ was that he indentified himself with sinners, and his justification of the godless formed the central core of the Gospel. This was the basis on which true and false spirits within the later tradition of the Church could be distinguished. So often ecclesiastical tradition had defended the position of the godly and pious, whereas Christ stood out as the justifier of the godless.

PART TWO

The Authority of Christ
in his Church

PAPER BY
DR E. KINDER

The English word "authority" has a wider meaning than the German "Autorität". In English translations of the Bible, ἐξουσία is rendered as "authority" whereas in German we translate it by "Vollmacht". The subject of this paper could equally well be formulated as "The Full Power of Jesus Christ in his Church" (*Die Vollmacht Jesu Christi in seiner Kirche*). This may make it a little clearer what kind of authority we are dealing with in this paper.[1]

The possessive pronoun in the wording of the title—"in *his* Church"—tells us that authority is here concerned with what is *his own*. The Church essentially is the Church ἐκκλησία τοῦ Θεοῦ ἐν Χριστῷ because she is constituted, inspired, ruled, and commissioned through Christ's redeeming action. The essential character of the Church does not allow of any other authority within her than that which Jesus Christ himself exercises through his redeeming action. "Thou only art the Lord." Jesus Christ alone is the living Head of the Church. All authority in the Church, if it is to be legitimate, must be legitimated through that authority which Jesus Christ himself exercises in the Holy Spirit. On this, I assume, we are fundamentally agreed.

What we have now to clarify concerns these three questions:

1. A preliminary question: In what does the authority of Jesus Christ really consist?
2. The main question: How is this realized in the Church?
3. How is this authority exercised practically in the Church?

[1] Cf. Karl G. Steck: *Recht und Grenzen kirchlicher Vollmacht*, Theol. Ex. 54, Munich 1956.

1. *The Nature of the Authority of Jesus Christ*

(*a*) The authority of Jesus Christ is wholly that of his saving action. This proves its authority through that inner power by which he saves men from error and doom, reconciles them to God the Creator, brings them to faith in God, and thereby liberates them unto salvation. He has authority as "the author and perfecter of faith" (Heb. 12. 2a). Jesus Christ has authority precisely in forgiving men their sin (Mark 2.5) and in bringing them into a final relationship with God as Father, through which they receive salvation.

He does this through his authoritative proclamation, that is, one uniquely authorized by God (Matt. 7. 29); yet even more through his entire being, by a life wholly emanating from God, as well as through his attitude, indeed most deeply of all through his self-giving ἀντὶ πολλῶν (Mark 10. 45). The authority of Jesus Christ is most of all that authority which springs from his self-giving for others so that they might be saved and brought to faith and thus obtain salvation.[2]

Thus the authority of Jesus Christ is of such a kind as forgoes the exercise of force or any sort of coercion in asserting and vindicating himself (cf. Matt. 26. 51-4). The only way in which his authority will assert and vindicate itself is through the power of his saving action which wins men from within, with the result that they acknowledge him as Lord on account of the deliverance they owe to him (cf. John 13. 13f). This authority then is not established by coercion but acknowledged from within. The "Kingly Rule of Jesus Christ" of which there is so much talk these days—talk which is all too hasty, rather unconsidered, and liable to be misunderstood—has the essential nature of rule in the sense of "dominium" in virtue of his self-giving towards those who have been saved and delivered by him, These now, from the experience of this deliverance, acknowledge him as their source of life. As

---

[2] Mark 10. 35-45, esp. vv. 42-5; Phil. 2. 6-11, esp. v. 9 διό. Cf. Luther, *Greater Catechism*, Explanation of the second article of belief (BS, pp. 651f): "What does this mean: 'becoming Lord'? It means a Redeemer . . . who has brought us from the devil to God, from death to life, from sin to righteousness and who keeps us there." The second article of the Apostles' Creed shows "what he has done and dared that he might win us and bring us under his *dominion*".

Luther says: "A Lord of life, of righteousness, of all that is good and blessed, who has taken us under His defence and protection to be His own, so that he may rule us through His righteousness, wisdom, power, life and blessedness." [3] This is not rule in the sense of "imperium", which is foreign rule exercised by external force.[4]

(*b*) Jesus Christ has this authority not by himself or in himself; rather, it is entirely the authority of the Son. This he has only because he lives and acts entirely as Son of the Father (cf. John 5. 19). The unique power of Jesus Christ consists precisely in his pointing away from himself and in his not desiring to be anything unless it be *from* the Father and *in relation to* the Father; in his living and acting wholly as one who is sent and empowered by the Father (John 4. 34; 8. 54; Matt. 17. 5); indeed, the only purpose of his life is to bring men under the authority of the Father (Phil. 2. 11 : Jesus Christ is "κύριος to the glory of God the Father"). The authority of Jesus Christ is grounded in his vindication of God's own essential authority — that of his redeeming and creative love (cf. Mark 2. 5, 7, 10f). God confirmed this authority of his Son by raising him (Acts 2. 36).

(*c*) Jesus Christ discharges his authority as Son also by making men aware of God's holy will and demand with all its radical implications.[5] This is the basis of the authority assigned to him as the final judge of all men (2 Cor. 5. 10). Furthermore, this authority of Jesus Christ is one that has been *given* to him (John 5. 26f). It is not an isolated authority, in the sense of "Christus legislator" — rather it serves the proper authority of Jesus Christ whose work is that of redemption. It is because the creative love of God as the heart of all things has been victorious in Jesus Christ that he has been given "all authority in heaven and in earth" (Matt. 28. 18): and it is because true manhood has been created through him alone that all human existence is ultimately judged by him (2 Cor. 5. 17; Eph. 2. 15). That is to say, only he who is inwardly and personally persuaded and convinced by the redeeming power of

---

[3] Op. cit., p. 652.

[4] Cf. W. Ehlert, "Regnum Christi" in *Zwischen Gnade und Ungnade*, Munich 1948, pp. 72-91.

[5] Cf. the ἐγὼ δὲ λέγω ὑμῖν in Matt. 5.

Jesus Christ and thus experiences his proper authority will acknowledge and submit to the juridical authority of Jesus Christ.

(Traditional dogmatics spoke of the dialectic between the "regnum gratiae" and the "regnum potentiae" of Christ during this age, both of which would merge into the "regnum gloriae" of the consummation.[6] It will be an important question for us to consider how the "regnum potentiae" of Christ is made real. But whatever our answer may be, it must be seen in its functional connection with his "regnum gratiae", which is the proper or characteristic authority of Jesus Christ.)

2. *The Realization of the Authority of Jesus Christ in the Church*

The main question of this paper is this: How does the authority of Christ, the character of which we have briefly described, become manifest in the Church?

Two main points need to be raised to this question.

(*a*) Jesus Christ empowers his disciples with his own authority: "As the Father has sent me, even so send I you" (John 20. 21b; cf. also John 17. 18). This is the fundamental meaning of "apostle". That authority which Jesus Christ has been granted as Son by the Father and which he wields in relation to the Father (see above), is now to be further exercised in his Name towards others by those whom he, on the strength of his redeeming work, has called to follow him. (Cf. Matt. 10. 1 and the whole of the chapter; Matt. 16. 18f; 18. 18; John 20. 22f, etc.[7])

(*b*) Yet, even allowing for all this authorization of the disciples to be apostles, the real and effective core of Jesus Christ's authority cannot be taken from him and transferred to others; nor can it be represented by them since Christ's origin from the Father, Christ's self-giving on the Cross, and God's ratification of his authority by raising him are utterly unique and cannot be transferred.

"Neither the soteriological nor the metaphysical series of biblical statements about Jesus Christ can be transferred into statements about the authority of the disciples as being those who are sent.

[6] Cf. the World Council of Churches' study theme on "The Kingdom of Jesus Christ in Church and World".

[7] See also Steck, op. cit., pp. 16f.

Here once and for all the words apply : Was Paul crucified for you ?
Or were you baptized in the name of Paul? (I Cor. I. 13)".[8]
Ultimately, therefore, the authority of Jesus Christ remains bound
to his own person. Raised and exalted, living and present, he is
himself the one abiding Head of his Church (Matt. 23. 8-10; 28. 20b;
Eph. 4. 15f). As such he desires to discharge his own authority in the
Holy Spirit through the service of the disciples : ὁ δὲ Κύριος τὸ πνεῦμά
ἐστιν (2 Cor. 3. 17). The authority which he grants to his disciples
only serves to bring men under his own authority as the living and
active Head of the Church (Eph. 4. 11f, 15f). For *this* authority
there can be no substitute. The authority entrusted to the apostles
stands for the abiding authority of Jesus Christ himself simply in
order that his authority may make itself felt (2 Cor. 4. 5; 5. 20).
Christ never completely gives away his authority to the disciples,
to the apostles, or to the Church, but in the Holy Spirit he keeps it
always in his own hands.

This compels us to view critically all ideas of Christ being fully
represented by the Church and of his authority being fully dele-
gated; the limitations of such ideas should be recognized.

(*c*) The fact that Jesus Christ himself desires to exercise his
authority for himself within his Church in the Holy Spirit does
not imply a "spiritualism" without contours or norms. Luther and
the Lutheran Confession emphasize vigorously that the Holy Spirit
desires to operate within the Church and for the Church through
such outward means as the spoken sermon and the physical actions
of the sacraments.[9] The authority of Jesus Christ is to be operative
through the Gospel, the substance of which is defined by the
apostolic κήρυγμα, going forth in proclamation and in the administration of sacramental acts, without "imprisoning" Christ and the
Holy Spirit within them.[10] (The purpose of the Reformation was to
assert the sole supremacy of the Gospel in the Church for the sake
of the sole supremacy of Jesus Christ.)

(*d*) The Gospel is to go forth within the Church and for the
Church through persons especially called to do this. This is shown
by the authorized apostolate at the original foundation of the

8 Steck, op. cit., p. 17.
9 *Augsburg Confession V*; Schmalkaldic Article III, IV, and VIII etc.
10 Cf. Steck, op. cit., pp. 18-20.

Church [11] (cf. 1 Cor. 12. 28-30; Eph. 4. 11f; 1 Cor. 4. 14-16; 11. 1; Luke 10. 16). Now, at the foundation of the Church the apostolate is unique and as such unrepeatable. Yet some element of it remains as an abiding feature of the structure of the ἐκκλησία of Christ, as both the Acts of the Apostles and the Pastoral Epistles frequently imply. This is why the Niceno-Constantinopolitan Creed confesses the abiding apostolicity of the Church, for this maintains the abiding authority of Jesus Christ in the Church. How the continuing apostolicity of the Church manifests itself is a controversial question. Different "Churches" give different answers to it. I should like to make these remarks:

1. In the first instance, the continuing apostolicity of the Church manifests itself in the *Apostolic Canon* of the New Testament (cf. Acts 2. 42a). By fixing the Canon of New Testament writings the Church of the second century acknowledged the fundamental principle of the Church that the Canon should serve as a norm for all later tradition. This does not imply a biblicist positivism; the authority of Jesus Christ has not passed into the literal text of the Bible. The authority of the New Testament Canon inheres rather in the original apostolic witness to the Gospel standing at the foundation of the Church, and this Gospel stands for the authority of Jesus Christ himself.

2. The apostolicity of the Church finds a further manifestation in the Apostles' Creed as being a summarized acknowledgement of the decisive core of Scripture. In making this confession, the Church answers and affirms the saving call of God; she speaks from her existential experience of the Gospel, as originally witnessed to in the New Testament, and from her decision of faith. Here one should speak of the graded authority belonging to ecclesiastical dogmas or Confessions of faith as *normae normatae*, which fall under the ultimate judgement of Holy Scripture as the *norma normans*. Used properly and in their right place, they too manifest something of the authority of Jesus Christ in the Church.

3. The Church's Ministry, too, as a "pastoral office" (1 Peter 5. 1-14) is intended to serve the effectual exercise of Jesus Christ's authority within his Church, and belongs therefore to the abiding apostolic

[11] See p. 38 above.

structure of the Church.[12] The reasons given here should be stressed: the Church's ministry serves the authority of Christ within the Church because the only basis for its constitution is that those who are entrusted with it preach the Gospel in accordance with the canon of the original apostolic κήρυγμα and administer the sacraments instituted by Christ. The authority of the ministry is functional and is dependent on the means of grace. Its claim rests on the authority of the means of grace and is bound up with them: it does not rest simply on the institution of the ministry as such. (Institutions in the Church can generally claim authority only in so far as they serve the means of grace and their prescribed purpose—never *per se* in a purely formal sense.)

4. The ministry of the means of grace and the pastoral ministry exist only for the sake of the Church as the congregation of believers (Eph. 4. 12), in order to magnify the authority of Christ within her. In all its activities the ministry is wholly directed towards the Church, the congregation. Moreover, it is grounded upon the *vocatio ecclesiae* (see above). Christ authorizes the whole Church as such to discharge and guard his authority. This is the basis for the Reformers' concept of the "general royal priesthood of all believers" (cf. 1 Pet. 2. 9; Rev. 1. 6). For this reason, Christ's call to enter the Church's office and ministries instituted by him is mediated through the whole Church.[13] The office of the ministry is not a function derived from the authority of the Church; rather, it is established by God in Christ through the Holy Spirit *for* the ἐκκλησία, as are all ministries within the Church (1 Cor. 12. 28-30; Eph. 4. 11f; Acts 20. 28). Yet the ἐκκλησία calls fit persons into this ministry entrusted to her. (The authority of the ministry cannot be derived from that of the Church nor, *vice versa*, can the authority of the Church be derived from that of the ministry. Each must be seen in its relative autonomy or independence, and each related to the other so as to act as a "brake" upon it, since each must be seen

12 Cf. *Apologia Conf. Augsburg* VII, 28, BS, p. 240: [*Ministri*] *repraesentant Christi personam propter vocationem ecclesiae, non repraesentant proprias personas, ut testatur Christi 'Qui vos audit, me audit'* (Luke 10. 16). *Cum verbum Christi, cum sacramenta porrigunt, Christi vice et loco porrigunt.*"
13 Cf. *Apologia Conf. Augsburg* XIII, 12, BS, p. 294: "*Habet . . . ecclesia mandatum de constituendis ministris quod gratissimum esse nobis debet, quod scimus Deum approbare ministerium illud et adesse in ministerio.*"

as being under the one authority of Jesus Christ, which together
they serve.) The "general priesthood" finds expression not only in
co-operating with the ministry of the means of grace or with the
pastoral ministry; it is seen in a great number and variety of
autonomous ecclesiastical offices and ministries (cf. 1 Cor. 12. 4ff).
As the bearers of these offices assemble in the supra-parochial
συνῳδός or (Latin) *concilium*, some part of the authority of Jesus
Christ within the Church and for the Church finds expression (cf.
Acts 15. 28). But just as the ministry of the means of grace and the
pastoral ministry in no way imply an institutional monarchism,
so this does not involve an autonomous democratism to which
Christ's authority is totally relinquished. Synod or Council, both of
which belong to the essential structure of the Church,[14] stand alike
under the authority of Jesus Christ himself. "There are varieties of
service, but the same Lord" (1 Cor. 12. 5). Both serve his authority
and, like the ministry of the means of grace or the pastoral
ministry, both are bound to the original apostolic κήρυγμα of the
Gospel and to the *regula fidei*; both are mutually related and
subordinate.

SUMMARY

Fundamentally speaking, the authority of Jesus Christ is realized in
his Church in four different special ways:

(a) In the Gospel as represented by the apostolic Canon.
(b) In the *regula fidei* of ecclesiastical dogmas or confessions of
    faith.
(c) In the ministry of the means of grace and the pastoral ministry.
(d) In the "general priesthood of all believers" as related to Synod
    or Council.

These four effective media stand in a graded scale of dignity: the
two latter, which share equal rank are of a more formal kind, and
stand below the two former. With none of these four, however,
can the authority of Jesus Christ be completely identified: his
authority surpasses all modes of its manifestation, and the four just
mentioned, graded in relation to one another, serve his authority

---

[14] Cf. H. Küng, "Structures of the Church", *Quaestiones disputatae* 17,
Freiburg 1962.

each in its own way without any one of them containing within itself the authority of Jesus Christ.

3. *The Exercise of Christ's authority in the Church*

We must now deal briefly with the question of how Christ's authority in the Church is to be exercised practically, in so far as we have the responsibility laid upon us to make it effective by our ministry through the media mentioned above.

Jesus Christ himself exercises his authority in the Holy Spirit; this authority in the strict sense of its purpose penetrates the means of its expression. Its intention, the purpose for which Jesus Christ claims any authority at all, is fulfilled where men are saved by him and have their sins forgiven, where they are reconciled to God by him, and brought to faith in God.[15] Consequently, the way in which Jesus Christ exercises his authority is by claiming our existential obedience to the will of God—in particular, obedience to the "new commandment" that we should love one another (John 13. 13-17, 34f). All ministerial service in the Church aimed at realizing Christ's authority must ensure that the Lord himself performs all that is essential and decisive, and that it is performed in such a way that other men will find faith. They must stand or fall before their Lord, and the claim of ecclesiastical authority, even that made in the Name of Christ, must not obtrude. Authority here can only mean *helping* a man's faith (cf. 2 Cor. 1. 24).

The authority of the Bible, of dogma, or of a confession of faith, as well as that of the Church in ministry and congregation, derived from the authority of Jesus Christ, must be seen within the bounds set by him who authorized them in the light of the purpose intended by him. Derived authority must remain subsequent to the goal for which it was intended to be authorized, and it must humbly defer final decision to him who authorizes and whom it must simply serve. Where people are concerned, this derived authority can only help them towards the threshold of faith : it has in principle to release them into freedom of faith and not keep them under tutelage. It can only admonish them to works of love in which faith finds practical expression; in this context nothing can be done by coercion.

This means that ecclesiastical authority may never cut itself loose from the functional obligation of serving the authority of

[15] See pp. 36-8 above.

Jesus Christ; it may not concentrate upon itself so as to claim a religious autonomy of its own. Church history shows the awful possibility that ecclesiastical institutions, originally established purely for the sake of the Gospel as its guardians and keepers, in the course of their development cut themselves loose from this functional obligation to the Gospel. They have come to claim an absolute autonomy or else have become subordinate to other motives. As a result, what was established as a safety-device outgrows its original function and now pretends to a religious authority of its own.

These principles concerning the application (*usus*) of the authority granted by Christ to the Church can now be exemplified in one or two particulars.

(*a*) According to the mind and intention of its Originator, ecclesiastical authority can only ever be discharged *non vi externa, sed verbo*. This *vis externa* which is to be rejected covers a fairly wide field, and includes all assertions of authority by way of external pressure, even pressures of a social kind. (When seen from the point of view of mass psychology, advertising too is a form of external pressure. It is a serious question how far the Church may use it in the service of exercising the authority entrusted to her.) In any case, what matters is always the authority appropriate to the matter we are dealing with : its peculiar character and proper autonomy may then be respected and not subjected to heteronomous principles.

The application of authority which corresponds to the saving Gospel of Christ can only be that of a personal appeal to heart and conscience. In principle, the Church has no other means at her disposal for asserting the true "substance" of her authority. She may use the means she has, with modesty but also with confidence, in the hope that the "substance" of her real authority will be proved in "demonstration of the Spirit and of power" (1 Cor. 2. 4), by saving men from perversity and existential guilt and by reconciling them to God so that they may receive salvation. All of the Church's authority, in serving the authority of Christ, must aim at calling forth and strengthening faith.

(*b*) All of the Church's authority, in serving the authority of Christ, must be concerned with the building up of the body of the faithful (1 Cor. 12. 4-7; Eph. 4. 11-13). Here she can but help and serve and, since this concerns life in the Spirit; she must not seek to coerce, control, or regiment. As she must always interpret her own authority as being derived from the saving authority of Jesus Christ, so she must also interpret it as aiming at the true life of the congregation in fellowship, love, and ἐυταξία.

The Church's responsibility and authority for calling men into the ministry—involving ordination, together with prior training and subsequent pastoral oversight—must also be discharged with a view to the building up of the body corporate. (The question arises through which particular agency—or agencies—this authority to govern the Church is actually discharged. According to Lutheran understanding, no direct *ius divinum* is laid down for this.)

(c) Another important question is whether, and if so in what sense, the Church's authority should also serve the authority of God's Law and whether the Church should also discharge her authority in a legal manner. Whatever the answer, her task can only be to magnify the Law of God. She can exercise "legal" authority only under these conditions :

(i) *non vi externa, sed verbo;* not through pressures but by appealing to heart and conscience;
(ii) by always serving the saving Gospel through which Christ rescues men, reconciles them to God, and incorporates them into the new fellowship of love.

One important example of this is the question of Church discipline, that is, exclusion from the congregation or from the ministry. This discipline is fundamentally necessary for the sake of the Church's own authenticity and the purity of her preaching.

(i) She cannot, however, resort to external means of coercion.
(ii) She must have the positive intention of winning the person back.
(iii) She can pass no ultimate judgements but must leave them to God.

The whole complex of Church law and its administration should also be considered here. Undoubtedly the view of Rudolph Sohm, reaffirmed by Emil Brunner [16] according to which the Church is a purely spiritual community devoid of any element of law, order, or institutions and according to which such elements imply a

[16] In *Das Missverständis der Kirche, Zurich* 1951.

fundamental alienation from the Church, is not correct. We must ask: On what theological principles is Church law based? Where are the limitations beyond which in consequence it becomes illegitimate? And how should it be properly administered?

Finally,

(d) Consequent upon the problem of "law" in the Church's authority, the question arises what authority the Church possesses over against the world. First and foremost comes the authorization to discharge her mission and her service of love (διακονία). The question remains whether, and if so in what sense, the Church should also assert the authority of Jesus Christ as the judge of mankind in the world; whether, that is, she should plead the case for man's humanity as such within the world — for humaneness, human dignity, the "rights of man", the preservation of mankind, and the right ordering of common life, etc. There can hardly be any question of "if". Much more difficult is the problem of *how* the Church may discharge her responsibility, and with it her authority in this direction. The kind of authority has to be regarded in its dynamic and eschatological aspect, that is, in its function of pointing towards the manifestation of Christ's Kingdom over the whole world.

DISCUSSION

FOLLOWING Professor Kinder's paper, the Bishop of Leicester (Dr R. R. Williams) opened the discussion. The Bishop said:

I must begin by expressing the thanks of the Conference to Professor Kinder for his very careful and typically thorough treatment of his subject. Many of us in England—at least those of us who are not professional scholars—stand amazed at the zeal and care with which our German colleagues approach any theological subject. They follow it through all its ramifications with unflagging energy. Relevant quotations from all parts of the New Testament spring apparently unbidden to their pens and tongues. The Pauline Epistles seem to have been written for the express purpose of providing them with relevant quotations. The whole mass of material falls naturally into shape, as though a matrix was waiting to receive the complex pattern, and to display the design already in their mind.

Such work has been put before us by Professor Kinder, and, speaking for non-academic circles in Britain, I fear that much of our work, when contrasted with German, must seem brief, casual, dilettante, and more strongly influenced by contemporary, empirical considerations than corresponding work in Germany would be.

It is not necessary to say that with much, if not all of Professor Kinder's paper, I should find myself in warm agreement. The close identification of Christ's authority with his redemptive, re-creative work is not unknown in our tradition. It was the main thesis of P. T. Forsyth's book *The Principle of Authority* (1913). It is clear that from an historical point of view, our Lord achieved his *dominium* over his Church through the Cross and Resurrection. Without these events there would have been no Church, and hence no authority of Christ in his Church. It is easy for us to agree that Christ's authority is addressed to the heart and conscience of man, and that it is not exerted in a compulsive, coercive sense. This was the theme of a great book by John Oman, *Vision and Authority*. We recognize that any authority that is exercised in accordance with God's will must be the authority of Christ himself, and that any exercise of authority apart from him and his will is a usurpation.

But in a conference of this kind, it is not necessary to mention

every point where we agree: there will be more ecumenical interest
and value if we mention those points where we might easily
diverge. I do not think this would arise because we disagreed with
anything that was said, but possibly because we might select
different points to stress, and because the final balance of our
pyramid of authority might be at a different point.

Now I notice in Professor Kinder's paper a very strong insistence
at all points on the direct, unmediated authority of Christ, and a
consequent tendency to limit very strictly any authority that
might be attached to any authoritative organs of Church life. Thus
Professor Kinder quoted "Qui vos audit, me audit", laying the accent
on the "me". When the Anglican hears those words, he hears the
accent falling on the "vos" — he sees in the saying a Dominical
sanction for the authority of the apostles and hence for the Church.
The Lutheran more naturally hears in it a warning that the apostles
must never speak except as the mouthpiece of their Lord.

Great care was taken not to allow any *independent* authority
to the Creed, to the pastoral office, or to decisions of the synods.
Now, while Anglicans would agree with the careful statements
made, their natural tendency would be to stress the other side of
the picture — that is, they would wish to teach that *through* the
organs of authority, through the Scriptures, through tradition,
through the ministry, and through the *consensus fidelium*, the
guiding, ruling hand of the Lord was actually at work.

There was a well-known saying of Archbishop William Temple
quoted by Archbishop Ramsey in *From Gore to Temple*:[17]

> When I consecrate a godly and well-learned man to the office and
> work of a Bishop in the Church of God, I do not act as a repre-
> sentative of the Church, if by that is meant the whole number
> of contemporary Christians; but I do act as the ministerial
> instrument of Christ in His Body, the Church. The authority by
> which I act is His, transmitted to me through His apostles and
> those to whom they committed it; I hold it neither from the
> Church, nor apart from the Church, but from Christ in the
> Church . . . This authority to consecrate and ordain is itself
> witness to the continuity of the life of the Church in its un-
> ceasing dependence on its Head, Jesus Christ, who is the same

[17] Op. cit., p. 125.

yesterday, today and for ever. Every priest who by virtue of his ordination celebrates the Holy Communion acts not for the congregation then present, nor for all Christian people then living on the earth, but as the organ of the Body of Christ, the ministerial instrument of Christ active in and through His Body; so that though no more than two of three persons be actually assembled, yet the congregation at that Holy Communion is the Communion of Saints, with which the persons present be they few or many, are there conjoined. Here, therefore, as in the Incarnation itself, we find the eternal in the midst of time, the secret of a fellowship against which the gates of death cannot prevail.

This is in my view a typically Anglican comment. It leaves the initiative, the *fons et origo* of authority where it belongs, in the hands of the Lord. But it accepts, gladly, and humbly, the fact that the ministry is there, an instrument of the Body, and for the Body, of the grace and authority of the Head.

I suspect that the historical situation of the Church of England may have influenced it in coming to lay stress on the divine authority which it believes works in and through it. Although never losing its predominant position among English religious communities, it has never had an unchallenged position. After the Reformation it had to concede a place to various kinds of nonconformists — Presbyterians, Independents, Baptists, and later Methodists. By the mid-nineteenth century, Rome was once more in the field, setting up her revived bishoprics. There was need in the Church of England for a sense of divine mission and authority, firmer and more visible than that in the nonconformist sects, but more controlled by Scripture and history than was that of the Church of Rome.

Perhaps you will forgive me if I mention two quite personal incidents which have a bearing on my theme. In 1957 I was Select Preacher before the University of Oxford. I had been a bishop for some four years, and I wanted to relate my sermon to the work which I was finding of such absorbing interest. I took as my text 2 Corinthians 13. 10: "The authority which the Lord gave me for building up and not for casting down." The sermon was afterwards published in *Theology* (February 1958) under the title "Apostolic

Principles and Episcopal Practice". I find in the sermon (which I had all but forgotten) these words:

> In one particular, for instance, St Paul's relation to the churches he visited was similar to that of a modern bishop. He represented an authority wider than that to be found in the local church. He checked their customs by those of "the churches of God" in a wider area, and their doctrine by the gospel which he had received. In the same way a bishop, with the authority of consecration, renewed by his regular meetings with the college of bishops, brings to the local church an authority with roots in the past and ramifications in the present. Like the great apostle, he has to take care to use his authority "for building up and not for casting down". The hasty or irresponsible word is long remembered, and he has to learn sometimes to keep silence even from good words, lest speaking unadvisedly with his lips he wound the weak or quench the smoking flax.

I think in that passage you can see how an Anglican bishop tries to think of his authority.

The other incident took place only recently, on last Easter Monday. In my diocese we had what seemed to us a wonderful Youth Rally, with fourteen hundred teenagers in a great tent, for an evangelistic and pastoral service. We had to help us a party of Gospel singers with guitars from a Baptist college. After the service I was thanking the Baptists for coming and they said: "We want to thank you—we are Free Churchmen, but we feel that to-day we have seen the authority of the Church at work, and we are rather impressed."

I could not refrain from asking myself afterwards what exactly it was that had conveyed this impression. The occasion was very informal, but I had asked them to put up their hands if they had received their Easter Communion. I had spoken to them plainly but I hope kindly on moral matters. I had tried to preach the Gospel to them. And with my staff in my hand I had given them God's blessing as they went off to their homes. All this was, I am sure, taken for granted among our Anglican members. But to our Baptist friends it was fresh, and they did not resent it. How far we are in the Church of England from being fit and ready for the Lord's use we know only too well. But this necessary penitence does not prevent us from feeling deep gratitude to God for what we believe are gifts he has given us. He has given us, often through what look to us the accidents of history, a balance, a proportion, which at its best enables the power of God to use the weakness of men as channels of his grace, to a degree for which we are humbly but truly grateful. It seems to us like that, but that is quite likely because we were born here, and brought up that way!

THESE COMMENTS by the Bishop of Leicester were followed by general discussion. All agreed how important it was to emphasize that the authority intrinsic to all Christ's work was that of his own Person: He is κύριος, his status is that of Son of God. The authority of his Person was apparent during his earthly ministry in his power to forgive sins, his right to cleanse the Temple, his teaching "as one having authority, not as the scribes".

At the same time Christ's function and status were felt to be rightly described in terms of service. Philippians 2 helps to provide material for the distinctively Christian definition of God.

It would be a mistake to speak of Christ only in relation to the Church, to redeemed humanity. Christ is also the *Logos* through whom creation is brought about (John 1; Col. 1; Heb. 1)—"by whom all things were made". Christ acts, therefore, in relation both to the natural creation and to the new creation. The writ of his authority runs in the κόσμος as well as in the ἐκκλησία.

LATER DISCUSSION on Professor Kinder's paper was opened by Dr Ernst Käsemann, who said:

During this conference we have experienced a wide measure of agreement on fundamentals in our conversations, yet it is the nuances, the differing perspectives and differently placed accents which demand our thought and attention. The question is how much latitude we are able and willing to allow one another. The statements I shall make will serve the purpose of determining this, as it were in an experimental way, in relation to Professor Kinder's paper. In this way the real point at issue in our problems will be clarified.

1. If I am not mistaken, the christological foundation and limitation of all ecclesiastical authority is as little in dispute amongst us as are the consequences resulting from it, namely that ecclesiastical

authority may be asserted only as a mode of self-giving. What we must now determine more precisely is the ecclesiological reality within which authority becomes, in a Christian way, possible, necessary, and authentic. This means that we are inquiring about the concrete expression of Christian authority, and that we are thereby contending that concrete authority and authorities are to be found where Christ reigns. No ministry, no χάρισμα, no office is without authority — that is, without the claim to be heard and heeded and without the right of offering, within its limits, encouragement, advice, warning, and criticism. Every Christian has such authority, wherever he is and whatever he does. That is why Ephesians 5. 21 demands that we should be subject to one another out of reverence for Christ.

The converse is also true: every office, every χάρισμα, every ministry, and every Christian has this authority only within the sphere of his service and in the exercise of it. The only fundamental and abiding measure of Christian authority is the breadth, depth, and determination of the service sustaining that authority. To define this statement more closely from an ecclesiological point of view, I would observe that without the general priesthood of all believers the Church does not seem to me to have apostolicity. Whatever the dangers of speaking of "Christ within us", this is something we cannot manage without when we are dealing with the validity and limitation of ecclesiastical authority. Otherwise all ministries would be in a vacuum, and that is not where Christ has placed us.

2.   Christ's authority in the Church loses its direction and purpose if one forgets that the will of God in Christ concerns not merely a religious community but the new world. Christ's authority in the Church is therefore an authority which sends the Church and her members into the world and lets them exist for the world (John 17). Otherwise it degenerates into the constitution of a religious group. Authority in the Church asserts the concrete claim of the predestined Cosmocrator who, according to the Declaration of Barmen (1934), leaves no department of this world without his promise and demand.

3.   At the same time this second statement must be qualified in two directions.

(*a*) Important as it is to see in Christ not merely the Lord of
Christian worship (*der Kultherr*) but also the Mediator of creation
and the Cosmocrator, it must not be forgotten that no christological
statement is legitimate which cannot be related to the Man on the
Cross. It is indispensable to relate all history to him and to say that
he brings with him the new creation—that is, new men and a new
humanity, united in peace and acting in solidarity. Yet this is
brought about, both in individuals and in the various Churches,
through Christ fetching back fallen Adam into the *nova obedientia*.
But this he can do only as the Crucified One. For only he, the
Crucified, places us in that ταπεινοφροσύνη which, whilst scorned
by Jews and Greeks alike, is the eschatological category of life
according to the will of God. Such lowliness is the anthropological
reflection of the event of the Cross.

(*b*) This means that Christ, because he is and remains the
Crucified, remains the Cosmocrator only in a secret, hidden, and
predestined way until the παρουσία. He rules the world not, as he
does the Church, directly by his Spirit but only and always through
his members—that is, through their discipleship, their service, their
proclamation of the divine will, their suffering, and the offence they
cause. The fact that he still deals with the world through men and
that his Spirit does not operate in the world without his disciples
corresponds with the Incarnation.

As all authority which is incompatible with the Cross is un-
christian, so all Christian authority is always open to the possibility
of contradiction since it can be asserted only by men to whose
service Christ has bound himself.

4. The qualifications of the previous statement determine the
character and limits of Christian authority, but do not invalidate
it. It was indispensable to emphasize the notion of "Christ in us" if
we were to take account of the Incarnation and the Cross. But it
is equally indispensable now to declare with similar firmness that
it is the rule of Christ which establishes and legitimates real and
concrete authority. Christ does not act in this world without us,
his disciples. Yet we are bound by his work, his will and, since this
is our only way of knowing them, by his Word. This Word is
beyond our control. We have no authority over it. It remains the
verbum externum, and accordingly the Church and the life of

the Christian can never be anything other than *creatura verbi*.

This also means that our service is not under our own control. We are responsible for it, yet we may not limit it or leave it undone as we think best. The power which has taken hold of us wants to demonstrate its power through us. Its Word is accompanied by signs and wonders. It puts men under unconditional obedience (ὑποταγή), and it effects this obedience through our service.

Accordingly the authority of Christ lays its demand precisely on believers. They are never discharged from the ranks of his regiment. The παραίνεσις of the New Testament—with its promise, consolation, exhortation, warnings, threats, judgement—is nothing but the expression of the claim of this authority. Christians and the Church never cease to remain in this age a part of the world. They must therefore become, again and again, that part of the world over which Christ's banner floats. This is not the work of the law, but the eschatological event through which Christ conquers the world. Thus the New Testament as a whole, and the Apocalypse with its letters to the Seven Churches in particular, show that this victory can also in fact mean destruction. The new creation always grows through judgement.

Christ does not act otherwise through his own in the world. God does not make alive without first killing, and only raises what is low. If we show the world the image of the Crucified, both as the law and promise of life, we cannot spare it offence nor ourselves avoid its curses and our own suffering. The Church's true authority grows in the shadow of the Cross; it is seen unmistakably in suffering; it cannot avoid the opposition of the world. For according to 2 Corinthians 2. 14ff, the Gospel brings about the division between the world of life and the world of death, and itself leads to life or death. He who is aware of this acts in his service as one who has behind him the most powerful and dangerous authority that exists, and he is bound to assert with fear and courage the claim of this authority on everyone; for otherwise he could not serve this Lord who is the hidden Cosmocrator.

PROFESSOR KASEMANN'S remarks were followed by general discussion, when a comparison was made between the *Pax Christi* and the *Pax Romana*. A similar atmosphere seemed to pervade both Virgil's Fourth Eclogue and St Paul's writings. All agreed that the authority of Christ was established wherever his members in this world concretely demonstrated humility before their brethren. The bearing of the Cross was always the means of establishing Christ's reign, and the task of the Church was to bear his Cross in this world. In this sense the Church was, therefore, both "institution" and "existential event" — two inseparable aspects of its existence.

The corporate nature of the Church as the vehicle of Christ's authority was then further discussed. In the Acts of the Apostles the κοινωνία of the Church was stressed (Acts 2. 42, etc.), and similarly St Paul emphasized the nature of the Church as being σῶμα. The New Testament also gives place to the notion of the Church as the New Israel. The teleological aspect of such ideas also finds expression : Scripture reminds us that the Church will become the Kingdom of God, and that in the heavenly city there will be no temple.

The constant tension within the life of the Church between her existence as a community and her service to the world was recognized by all. So was the tension between the institutional and existential or functional aspects of her life.

FURTHER DISCUSSION was opened by Canon S. L. Greenslade, who said :

Besides the discussions, both wide and deep, which we have been having on the nature of authority, I think we should give some time to the authority of the Ministry, a theme which could divide our Churches and is always difficult in ecumenical conversation. I confess that I find it much easier to talk about ministers as servants than to understand, much less define, their authority; but the subject cannot be evaded. For the moment I want to open up a single line of approach to the question, which is of course not the only one. And I start from what I expect will be common ground for us : that the Ministry is, on New Testament evidence, a "given" element in the life of the Church. I shall state my line of thought rather abstractly, but I believe that it arises from reflection upon the New Testament situation.

I start from the New Testament picture of the Church, in which, apart from the Apostles, and perhaps even in their case, *functions* are more evident and more definite than *offices*. Preaching, teaching, healing, pastoring, supervising, ministering sacraments, etc., have to be done for the building-up of the Church.

Some men are given special responsibilities within the whole community, not necessarily permanent, but tending to become permanent. These are in principle duties, charges, services to be rendered; but they lead to a kind of authority, for within the community *these* are the men responsible to Christ for doing certain things — that is, they are authorized for these functions. Such functions are always to be discharged in love, as service; but this is not incompatible with authority. A judge serves the community as being an authority on law and exercising authority in matters of law. The Pope, as understood by Roman Catholics, is *servus servorum Dei*.

Thus the duty to discharge functions gives rise to rights, though only in the sense that other members of the community have a duty towards these ministers: the duty to allow them to give their particular service. There is a system of reciprocal rights and duties within a fellowship (which, in history, is never a perfect fellowship. The balance is often disturbed.)

Even if historically the order of sequence is (*a*) function and responsibility, leading to (*b*) office and authority, yet once the offices exist and have become recognized elements in the life of the Church, men are directly appointed to the office in order to perform the functions. They are given status. It becomes a matter for discussion whether they cannot or should not perform the particular, recognized functions or cannot perform them with authority without the office or status.

The ultimate giver of authority is Christ. Now, although there are senses in which Christ gives himself to his people, he does not, in commissioning his ministers, make them to be himself or hand over his own authority to them as their possession. Nevertheless, they are not things or functions but persons, authorized to discharge functions for him as persons. They have become, I suppose, through their commission a particular kind of person. In other words, we cannot set aside the question what *ordo* or *sacerdotium* is: we have to examine the term disliked by many, "character", even "character *indelebilis*".

We have to examine concretely how this office or status is acquired and to ask whether and on what grounds we can distinguish the special ministers and their special, proper functions. Anglicans tend to be interested in ministers as duly authorized ministers of sacraments, essentially so as to be sure that the sacraments themselves shall operate with the authority and efficacy of Christ. In this respect, ministers do not exactly exercise authority *over* laymen, unless the administration of sacraments is linked to a disciplinary system. In respect of the ministry of the Word, the objectivity or authority is again, in principle, in the Word itself, and the minister is servant. But is his special service here divinely assisted in any particular way which imposes a duty upon others to hear him, to accept what he says, or to obey him? Is there a *magisterium*?

One comes round inevitably to the usual questions, such as the nature of ordination; and this must bring in the special question of the Apostles and whether, or in what sense, they have successors, and what the authority of such successors would be. However, behind any matters which are controversial as between Churches, there is the question common to all of us who have an ordained ministry. Ministers are servants, first and last; but in what proper senses have they authority? And what duties, if any (considered theologically, not just constitutionally), have the laity towards them? The approach through consideration of a system of mutual rights and duties sounds legalistic, and must not be taken in a merely sociological fashion. The question is what Christ does to persons whom he specially calls for special services.

In the brief discussion which followed this paper, the attention of German delegates was drawn to the wording of the formula used in the Ordination of Priests according to the Book of Common Prayer: "Take thou authority to preach the Word of God and to minister the Holy Sacraments in the Congregation where thou shalt be lawfully appointed thereunto."

Through shortage of time, there was no opportunity to develop the points raised by Canon Greenslade.

PART THREE

The Authority of the
Church To-day

CANON I. T. RAMSEY

In writing this paper I have been very conscious of the unbeliever looking over my shoulder, and if it seems at points to stray very far from theology my defence would be that I am haunted by the point which concluded one of our recent discussions—namely that the Church often seems very distant from the contemporary world, and devoid of any authority for it. Perhaps the most charitable view to take of the defects of this paper is indeed to see it as an attempt to hold together in thought Christian ideas about the Church on the one hand, and the attitudes and approaches of the contemporary world on the other. What I hope to do is first to say something about the concept of authority in general. I am very conscious that this part of the paper may seem very difficult if not irrelevant. But, as I hope to show, it is an essential background for what I say in the second part of the paper about the problems and difficulties which are raised when we wish to speak to-day of the authority of the Church.

I

In discussing the concept of authority in general I shall formulate some distinctions in the hope that they may clarify in some degree what is an exceedingly tangled topic, and with the same intention I shall also discuss one or two of the basic questions which any appeal to authority necessarily involves. For instance: Do all true beliefs, or only some, involve an appeal to authority—if only some do, are these inevitably suspect? Does an appeal to authority necessarily compromise personal freedom or intellectual integrity? When does the authoritative become the authoritarian? Or again, we may ask whether an appeal to authority involves some claim that the authority is infallible. Can something both be taken as authoritative and yet acknowledged to be fallible? With these and similar questions in mind let us now pass to our general discussion of authority which will, as I say, prepare the way for our later discussion of the authority of the Church.

To speak of A in certain circumstances being an "authority" is to recognize in A and to ascribe to A, at least in those circumstances, power—power to promote in some degree a particular conclusion or particular behaviour. There seems to be no limit as to what A may be. For instance, A may be a person. He may be an expert who by his knowledge and training is specially qualified to deal with particular problems of thought or behaviour—the classical scholar, the medical consultant, the headmaster, the psychiatric social worker. He may be a monarch or president, a prime minister, an ambassador, a vice-consul—all those who, as it would be said, are set in positions of authority, who display civil or political power. He may be a friend whose love or concern inspires us, or who influences us by his example or his counsels. Here in fact we see something of the distinction Professor Kinder was drawing between *imperium* and *dominium*. On the other hand, A may be an inanimate object as when we speak of the authority of a book, or of a document, for example, the Bill of Rights, or of a flag. Besides which, people have spoken, for example, of the authority of Reason, sometimes having in mind that by which the spirit of a man could be characterized; at other times interpreting it in terms of that compelling power which an argument possesses when no one who deserves to be called reasonable can avoid following it to its conclusion. Moral philosophers, like Butler and Kant, have also spoken of the authority of conscience and of the Moral Law. Christians have appealed in particular to the authority of Jesus, of the Scriptures, or of tradition, to the authority of a priest or bishop; they have also appealed to revelation, to the "Word of God", to Creeds, to defined doctrine, to Articles, to some Church order or institution, to a liturgy or Prayer Book—to some or all of these as being "authoritative".

In all this complexity we can at least be confident that there is no one thing called "authority" which all these diverse objects possess as a common attribute, yet I think that talk about transferring "authority" is sometimes construed on that basis. We shall certainly reach no clarity on that supposition; on the contrary, discourse about "authority" must be one of the most likely

candidates to benefit from an application of Wittgenstein's slogan —
"Don't look for meanings, look for use". Be alert to contexts!

What will emerge, I hope, from my discussion is that there are
prima facie two different contexts in which the word "authority"
can be set; that these contexts spread from two different, metaphysical, presuppositions. These presuppositions need not be incompatible, but contemporary society has an overriding preference
for one presupposition rather than the other, and of the two, it is
the one to which least justice can be done to the Church as a
distinctively Christian community. Further, Christian discourse
itself often incorporates both views, while failing to distinguish
between them.

Let us try then to keep as alert as we can to the different
contexts in which authority is spoken of, and to try to get some
order into what seems to be a conceptual tangle. Let us consider
these distinctions :

(*a*) The distinction between "belief on evidence" and "belief on
authority";
(*b*) The distinction between "primary" and "secondary" authorities;
(*c*) The distinction between the authority of a fact (in a sense to be
elucidated) and the authority of a person (also in a sense to be
elucidated).

(*a*) *Belief on evidence and belief on authority*
Belief or behaviour based on authority has often been contrasted
with belief or behaviour based on evidence. Indeed, for some this
is the fundamental distinction between a religious and a scientific
attitude, and I do not need to remind you how much the scientific
attitude dominates the contemporary world, and that the Christian
ignores it at his peril.

But the distinction between belief on evidence and belief on
authority is by no means as clear cut as it might seem. To see how
the distinction becomes blurred, let us notice that in the case of any
belief *p*, we may *prima facie* distinguish :

(i) The way by which we came to believe *p*.
(ii) The means by which we would now justify believing *p*.
(iii) What *p* is about.

Now we may grant that for some beliefs, these three features

5

virtually collapse into one, and this is most clearly the case with elementary scientific beliefs, which constitute the most important example of belief on evidence. For example, suppose that on the basis of taking a tripod, porcelain triangle, bunsen, crucible, and blue copper sulphate we believe p, that blue copper sulphate turns white on heating. Here is the way by which we have come to believe p. To justify p now would be to arrange a repeat performance; and the centre-piece of this repeat performance, as of the original experiment, is what p is about. Here is one of the simplest, and clearest possible examples of belief on evidence, and such scientific beliefs are often regarded as the ideal and paradigm of all belief—what is called "letting the facts speak for themselves". Here, it might be said, there is no element of belief on authority. But how did we know that the blue crystalline solid was copper sulphate? Presumably, we believed this on the authority of the label on the bottle—and even though this might be converted to a belief on evidence by subjecting the blue solid to chemical analysis, it seems unlikely that an element of authority could ever in practice disappear altogether, and perhaps it could never disappear in theory either since we accept a common language by which to make communication possible. So there seems to be no belief on evidence devoid of all appeal to authority.

As a second example, suppose I believe that a train leaves Oxford for London at 8.52 a.m. Presumably, I believe this on authority, the authority of the Western Region time-table of British Railways; but the means by which I could justify this belief, and what the belief is about is in the second case a different matter altogether; it is a matter, not of authority but of evidence— the kind of evidence that would become available if I stood on the Oxford railway platform one morning about ten minutes before nine o'clock. Here to put it crudely, we have authority and evidence fairly evenly mixed.

Thirdly, suppose I believe that "whosoever will be saved: before all things it is necessary that he hold the Catholic faith". It is likely that I have come to believe this on the authority of the so-called Athanasian Creed, and if I were asked to justify this belief now, either I could say that this authority was final and ultimate when there could be no question of justifying an ultimate authority (for that would be to search for something more ultimate than the ultimate), *or* I could show how the belief followed from taking certain biblical passages as authoritative. It might seem that this was a belief wholly on authority; but presumably even here it would have to be allowed that certain future events at any rate could count as evidence for or against the belief, for what the belief is about (namely, salvation) is something for which there will be, according to the *Quicunque vult*, unmistakable future evidence. "Which Faith except every one do keep whole and undefiled : without doubt he shall perish everlastingly." Incidentally, other questions of evidence would also arise around the biblical passages. But undoubtedly the element of authority here is high.

What now have these examples shown? First, that there is no simple contrast between "belief on evidence" and "belief on authority". No example has been found in which a belief was entirely the one or entirely the other, though the examples have shown, I hope, that the elements of evidence and authority admit of the widest possible variations. Nor need we suppose that these elements of evidence and authority vary inversely, though my examples may have suggested that.

To guard against that misunderstanding let us notice, secondly, that though the phrases "belief on evidence" and "belief on authority" are verbally parallel, the contrast they draw is not one between two species of belief. It is true that the phrases may be said to tell of two different ways in which we come to believe *p*. But the ways are so different as to set the phrases in a total imbalance. Belief on evidence is an *epistemological* matter; belief on authority is, so far at least, a *sociological* matter. So the contrast can better be expressed as a contrast between

(i) the way in which at any rate some beliefs are evidenced and justified.
(ii) the way in which beliefs are transmitted.

To speak of holding a belief *p* on authority is thus to acknowledge our dependence on some agent or other means — animate or in- animate — for transmitting the belief to us.

On the other hand, it has sometimes been argued that beliefs on evidence, besides involving an appeal to authority in the way the examples have shown, do not escape being beliefs on authority, for the ultimate authority for holding such a belief must be the evidence which verifies it.

The point has been expressed otherwise by distinguishing between a primary and a secondary authority in relation to every belief, and to a discussion of this distinction we now turn.

(b) The distinction between "primary" and "secondary" authorities

It has sometimes been said that in relation to any belief *p* we must distinguish between the *primary* authority, namely, what verifies *p*, what *p* is about, and *secondary* authorities, namely, various means which we acknowledge as reliable and trustworthy for expressing or transmitting *p*.

Examples will make the distinction tolerably clear. The easiest case is a news item such as the recent earthquake in Alaska. The primary authority for the belief that most of the buildings in the main street of Anchorage had collapsed in an earthquake is in fact the collapsing buildings in the Anchorage street at the time of the earth tremor; the secondary authorities are the seismograph records, newspaper photographs, broadcast reports, and the like.

In some ways historical studies, though they lead to various complications, may be thought to supply us with the best examples, because here secondary authorities abound. Indeed, it is very often the case that one of the functions of historical studies is to make such a comparative assessment of secondary authorities as to reach that which most reliably tells us "what happened". For obvious reasons we cannot normally in history have direct and independent access to a primary authority. So, if we are interested in the actual battle of Naseby, while our primary authority will be what happened on 14 June 1645 in those fields in hilly country between Daventry and Market Harborough, this is inevitably elusive and only approached by means of secondary authorities such as the letter written by Oliver Cromwell to Mr Speaker Lenthall from Market Harborough on 14 June 1645 after the battle had been won. On the other hand, this letter, once its genuineness and authenticity have been established, is a primary authority for the civil war which included its writing amongst the significant events which constituted that historical unit, though the monument and obelisk on the field of battle are secondary authorities for *both* the battle *and* the Civil War.

Thirdly, the primary authority for believing that the square on the hypotenuse of a right angled triangle is equal to the sum of the

squares on the other two sides is this proposition seen as the conclusion of an argument in Euclidean geometry, and the secondary
authority is the argument which transmits it.

In these examples, then, we have noticed that while there can
be many diverse authorities—records, photographs, persons, written
documents, stone monuments, arguments, and so on—all these are
for the most part secondary authorities—witnessing to and transmitting a primary authority which so far is the authority of a
"fact". Further, that which determines whether or not secondary
authorities such as records, photographs, or persons are reliable, will
be the "facts" with which they accord or discord. Here is supposed
to be a firm, indubitable basis, a solid foundation for all else; and the
basis is given a quasi-religious status. Such facts, we are told, "are
sacred", even though "comment is free"; and when, as we remarked
earlier, people talk of letting "the facts speak for themselves", there
is thereby attributed to the facts some sort of self-authenticating
character.

Indeed, taking our two sections together, it looks as if there is
nothing unreasonable about an appeal to authority provided that
the final word lies with the facts. But now two difficulties arise
which I propose to discuss in a third section.

(c) *The authority of a fact and the authority of persons*
What of these facts which are given a quasi-religious status? It is
true that we do not usually speak of the "authority" of a fact. But
Bertrand Russell certainly supposed his sense-data to be authoritative facts when he took them as the "solid basis" for knowledge.[1]
And whether Hume is consistent or not in his discussion of miracles,
he certainly presupposes that there can be no authority greater than
that of a "fact".

This leads straight to our first difficulty. In recent years we have
come increasingly to recognize that the very concept of an isolated,
independent, self-authenticating fact is bogus. We might easily have
realized this if we had ever asked ourselves the question: Is it a
"fact" that the sun rotates around the earth? We see it move with
our own eyes; here is something "given" if anything is. But all of us
would say rather that in fact the earth rotates around the sun,
showing how much questions of fact are interwoven with a

[1] *Problems of Philosophy*, p. 30.

conceptual scheme. Facts have no authority apart from the conceptual scheme with which they appear.

If you think this is an extravagant claim, let two of my philo- sophical colleagues make the same point in a different way.

Mr J. R. Lucas writes:

> . . . there are no basic facts: there are only facts relative to a dispute. Since there is nothing that cannot on some occasion be reasonably doubted, there can be no truths established beyond doubt to all comers, no elemental facts which we just have to accept and on which all else is based. Nothing is never doubtful, though this is not to say that everything is always doubtful. In every dispute we have to start somewhere, though there is no- where that is the starting point for every dispute.
>
>   This is a little too strong: though there is nothing we *cannot* doubt, there are many things that, apart from our metaphysical moments, we *do not* doubt: there is a core of accepted truths that are unquestioned by all people living at a given time, and unquestionable by any reasonable man at that time, not engaged in philosophy; and on these established platitudes, accepted by the many though not by the philosophers, we can base all our reasonable and practical contentions. These facts, adequate for our non-philosophical constructions, prove, however, shifting sands when we try to build a theory of knowledge or theory of truth upon them: because then we try to have our facts as basic facts, neutral elemental atoms, facts not with regard to this or that specifiable issue, but with regard to any conceivable issue; facts not in the context of a dispute between two actual or likely disputants, but in the context of any argument between any pos- sible disputants whatsoever, or rather, facts in no context at all. We think too much of facts as hard, brute facts, existing inde- pendently of us and ineluctable, as things that are what they are, and whose consequences will be what they will be, and about which we must not seek to be deceived. Having hypostatised them we bow down to them, and prostrate ourselves before them. It is unnecessary. It is impossible. Facts are not sacred: they are not worth worshipping: they do not exist: they are not even things.[2]

2 In *The Philosophical Quarterly* (April 1958) Vol. 8, No. 31, p. 156.

Earlier Mr Lucas has made a point very relevant to our present theme:

> I can conclude that King John was a much maligned patriot or Richard III a sensitive soul sincerely anxious for the welfare of his wards: if I do, I cannot be dismissed out of hand, as I can if I think that Magna Carta was issued by Charlemagne, or the battle of Bosworth was a naval victory of Drake's. In each case we are contrasting the sort of statement where there is latitude and two well-informed and honest men could reasonably differ, with the sort of statement where the external controls are much more rigid, and where a man cannot have an opinion of his own without thereby revealing himself either unreasonable or dishonest. But, and this is the important point, the connection goes in the opposite way to what we thought it did. Facts do not make the reasonable man, the reasonable man makes the facts.[3]

The reasonable man is not worshipping the facts: he is acknowledging the authority of a standpoint, of a certain view of the world which is "unquestioned by all people living at a given time, and unquestionable by any reasonable man at that time".

Likewise, Mr R. M. Hare in his essay on "Religion and Morals" writes: "People sometimes talk as if facts were somehow given us entirely independently of any dispositions of our own with regard to them. Kant saw that this is not so .... with principles of some sort we do not get any facts; there is no distinction between fact and illusion for a person who does not take up a certain attitude to the world",[4] and he continues later: "Certainly it is salutary to recognise that *even* our belief in so-called hard facts rests in the end on a faith, a commitment, which is not in or to facts, but in that without which there would not be any facts." [5]

Here is Mr Hare pointing us not to facts as authoritative, but to whatever it is which calls from us "faith" in, or "commitment" to a certain understanding of the universe.

There, then, is the first difficulty about taking facts as authoritative. The discussion of the second difficulty now takes these reflections further. For even if we were led, as originally we were, to

3 Ibid., p. 153.
4 In *Faith and Logic*, ed. B. G. Mitchell, p. 190.
5 Ibid., p. 192.

the point of thinking that all ultimate authority resided in facts, we should now have to grant that there are many other primary "authorities", authorities for which an ultimate claim is normally made, which nevertheless would not be called "facts", as we have been using that word.

For instance, monarchs, ambassadors, prime ministers, bishops, vice-consuls, sergeant-majors, headmasters possess authority *as such*. A person by displaying his behaviour pattern — when he has been appropriately commissioned — thereby and in so doing exercises authority: The act of commissioning is a transfer of authority: "Ex auctoritate mihi commissa, admitto te . . . ." and he who is admitted becomes himself authoritative in a way he was not already.

This is an authority such as is attributed to the Moral Law, and it is in terms of this concept of authority that we might speak of the authority of conscience or the authority of revelation once we were agreed about what the words "conscience" or "revelation" referred to.

So the concept of authority belonging to a person as one trans-missive agent amongst many, which attributes ultimate authority either to "facts" or, better, to agreed conceptual schemes held as part of one's commitment to the universe, has to be supplemented by the concept of authority inhering in a person, and this authority is exercised when the person is active, and in particular when he is active in a certain rôle. A person may in this sense be a primary authority, and when he is, it is not the primary authority supposed to characterize a fact, or ascribed to facts in a conceptual scheme: it is a primary authority intuited in a vision, declared in a disclosure.

It was Bishop Berkeley who argued in effect that such a disclosure of ourselves as comes in activity is that which is most characteristic of a person, a disclosure of ourselves as most characteristically personal, and not of ourselves as a mere assemblage of facts. Says Euphranor, "By the person Alciphron is meant an individual thinking things, and not the hair, skin, or visible surface, or any part of the outward form, colour or shape, of Alciphron" [6], and later, "An agent therefore, an active mind or spirit, cannot be an idea, or

[6] *Alciphron, Dialogue IV. 5.*

like an idea" [7], and Berkeley's use of the word 'idea' is very like the contemporary use of the word "facts". So we may claim the support of Berkeley for the conclusion, which in the present context I will state rather than argue, that this disclosure of ourselves is a disclosure of our transcendence, indeed of our mystery — what we are more than the facts, more than the social pattern in terms of which our activity is expressed, and to which transcendent activity our social behaviour points as a sign, token, and symbol. A person in this sense makes a transcendent claim on us when we intuitively acknowledge as a primary authority some active aspect of his personal life, for example, his loving us.

The leading question with which I now conclude this first and longer section of my paper is this: "What understanding do we have of what we take to be our basic Christian authority? There are two possibilities:

(*a*) It may be the authority of facts in a conceptual scheme. On this view, an appeal could be made to both Scripture and Tradition as basic authorities whose mutual relationship would then have to be elucidated. But the Church would only have the secondary authority of a transmitting agency.

(*b*) Alternatively it may be an authority something like that which breaks in on us when a person discloses himself to us, for example in love, as the person he is. On this view Scripture, Tradition, and the Church would all be tokens and expressions of the disclosure which, arising around them, was a disclosure of God's activity in Christ. Indeed, each would be an expression of that challenge and reaction which Dr Greeven mentioned as necessary for an understanding for all authority, and which, I would say, every disclosure presupposes.

Perhaps there was something of these two possibilities in Dr Käsemann's mind when he distinguished between the formal expression of an authority and the authority of charismata. At any rate, of the phrases we have used to point to a basic authority some would be equally at home in either of the contexts we have distinguished, for example, the "Evangelium", the "Kerygma", the "Magisterium", the "Depositum Fidei", the "Gospel of Christ", the

[7] *Alciphron, Dialogue VII. 5.*

"Mind of Christ", and the "Scriptural Deposit", though it is possible that the phrases "Depositum Fidei" and the "Scriptural Deposit" are phrases which belong more naturally to the first context. At the same time three phrases we have used point unmistakably to the second context, for example, Professor Kinder's phrase when he spoke of the "authority of Christ as addressed to the heart", a *dominium* not an *imperium;* the "impact of the Christ event", and the "impressiveness of Christ's person". Again Dr Greenslade's use of the concept of duty and correlative rights to elucidate Christian authority points in the same direction.

2

Before passing to a discussion of how these general considerations bear on the authority of the Church, let me now take up two of the questions I raised at the start.

First, is an appeal to authority reasonable in the matter of belief or behaviour? We saw that there was probably no belief which did not involve an appeal at least to some secondary, transmissive authority which we were prepared to take as reliable. Further, we saw that the appeal to facts as sacred scarcely concealed an authority which it implicitly acknowledged, for it involved a commitment to a standpoint or perspective on the world which arose as a response when, in some way or another and through a conceptual scheme, the world made an authoritative claim upon us. In this way, indeed, even in the earlier case, we were brought close to a concept of authority which regards authority as inhering in (say) a person or the Moral Law. This view of authority was the second case we examined, when some particular belief about a person, or some particular behaviour, arises from and within the commitment which is called from us as a spontaneous response when we acknowledge the authority of that person or of the Moral Law respectively. In various ways, then, an appeal to authority runs through the whole pattern of belief and behaviour and is reasonable precisely in being so wide-spread and ubiquitous.

Secondly, how far does an appeal to authority compromise our freedom or integrity?

I do not think that much reassurance about freedom will be needed, provided we have the second context for authority. For it is precisely in responding to the kind of authoritative challenge which inheres in the love of a person or in the obligability which is expressed in the Moral Law that we are distinctively persons, Here is the familiar theme of John Oman's *Vision and Authority*. Indeed, it is only those who have the first context for authority and *in its undeveloped form*, those who worship facts, whose freedom and personality are compromised. For, like everyone else, they match what they worship and become prisoners in an inert, lifeless world which stares them ruthlessly in the face.

Nor will our intellectual integrity be compromised by an appeal to authority once it is recognized that the authoritative is not co-terminous with the unquestionable or the infallible. This will be readily agreed about secondary authorities. For example, I take the railway time-table as authoritative about the facts of railway journeys but, if I am wise, I hardly ever assume it be infallible and unquestionably correct. Again, in the other context for authority, while many people would take conscience as authoritative for moral behaviour, they would not suppose that the "deliveries" of conscience were infallible. We may all recognize the authority of Duty, without implying that a judgement about a particular duty is infallible. Does this mean, then, that it is to primary authorities that we must look for a combination of authority and infallibility?

Someone like Russell, for whom "facts" were primary, certainly supposed that there were infallible protocol sentences wich lay at the heart of all reliable language; and it might be claimed for Descartes that in self-disclosure he knew infallibly that he existed. It looks at first sight that both contexts for authority trade in infallibilities.

Certainly the first does, but there is no question of integrity being compromised because everyone who utters a protocol sentence is aware at the same time of the evidence which verifies it. There is no unquestioning acceptance, on authority, of an assertion in whose verification we have no interest.

What of the second context? Does this deal in infallibilities? We have seen that whatever is given to us in this context as a primary authority is discerned and acknowledged by an intuition; in this way, primary authorities are disclosed in some kind of vision. But intuition never brings with it a pattern of discourse whose infalli-bility is guaranteed. Disclosures, as authoritative, make an acknow-ledged claim on us; but this claim can only mistakenly and deceptively be translated into apparently infallible expressions. For instance, in the case of the Cartesian "I exist", we might seem to have an infallible expression of a disclosed authority. But it is a notorious commonplace that Descartes gained this infallibility only at the cost of insuperable problems about the relations between "I" and "exist" in using these words as used in ordinary discourse. In short, if authoritative insights are assumed to yield infallibilities, these apparently infallible assertions are empirically compromised. Or to express it differently, if authoritative insights are not to be worthless, they must suffer the necessary indignity of being translated into corrigible assertions.

Meanwhile, what we must not do is to suppose that when a primary authority is given in a disclosure, there comes with it a given label as well, an expression whose infallibility is self-guaranteed. We must not confound insight and the expression of that insight; we must distinguish between a disclosure and our understanding of what the disclosure discloses. To talk of A being an "infallible authority" may be a way—albeit misleading—of giving a slant on, and pointing to, the acknowledged total claim which A makes on us. But even to allow with caution that way of talking does not at all license us to have infallible assertions. To suppose so is to make a severe verbal skid and to generate uncontrolled, directionless talk by failing to distinguish what is logically diverse—namely, insight on the one hand, and the expression of an insight on the other.

Intellectual integrity will certainly be compromised if ever we allow ourselves to assume that a particular expression of an authority is infallible, so that there is no need to test that expression for adequacy and reliability. To suppose that an expression can carry with it the claim of the authority it explicates is to attribute to a proposition a feature which can only belong to what the proposition speaks of: it is to commit, as we said earlier, the blunder of confounding insight and its expression. So an appeal to authority need never, and will not, compromise personal integrity providing that we do not assume that some expression of that authority is infallible and beyond question. Further, it is only when an appeal to authority compromises personal freedom or integrity that it can be called "authoritarianism", and on the analysis I have been putting forward this would only arise if, on the second view, we chose to call infallible one amongst the various possible explications which may be offered of a disclosed authority.

Let us now see the bearing on the authority of the Church to-day of these considerations about authority in general.

Our discussion has suggested two different contexts in relation to which we may understand the authority of the Church.

On the first view — that which takes facts as authoritative, as being the primary authority for all reliable assertions — the Church is seen as one social institution amongst others, as a social group having its own distinctive organization, its distinctive officers and membership rules, and existing to purvey certain facts. On this view, the Church is thus a secondary authority in relation to a primary authority made up of the "facts" of the Gospel and for whose transmission it exists. As such a secondary authority, the Church is the more reliable a transmitter the more continuous it is a social group, and the more it is a harmonious social group. We are all accustomed to think of the old-established firm, with happy staff relations, being of all firms the most reliable in the claims it makes for what it purveys.

At the same time, it is only one amongst other secondary authorities of which for example the Bible is obviously another. For on this view the Bible also exists as a transmitter of those "facts" which are the primary authority of the Christian faith. The relation between these two secondary authorities of Bible and Church is something quite external as we see it expressed in the old maxim: "The Bible to teach, the Church to guide".

This is a view of the Church and its authority which has an obvious appeal to an age which is empirically minded. The Church is one society amongst others, and like all social groups it has its imperfections. At the same time however, there is no *logical* reason why it should not be perfectly reliable, giving an exact and unambiguous account of the facts supposed to be the primary authority. In this way, and on this view, it is logically possible for the Church as for the Bible to be infallible yet not authoritarian.

When we considered Oliver Cromwell's letter after the battle of Naseby, we saw how one and the same document, in two different though not necessarily entirely diverse contexts, could have respectively primary and secondary authority. Equally so, while the Church is a secondary authority in relation to the "facts" it transmits, as a social institution it is a primary authority in its own right. It has the status of a fact. So the Church can possess authority simply because of its size, of its wealth, of its business efficiency, or of its impressive public relations. I think that it is in such terms, and only in such terms, that the authority of the Church is often measured by our contemporaries and (I need hardly say) generally found wanting. Nor are these contemporaries all unbelievers. They number amongst them all those who are appalled by our ill-distribution of man-power, the lack of any general executive staff, and so on. Contrariwise, there are many for whom the authority of the Church of England has clearly increased because its investment policy has been so strikingly successful. Again on this view, a bishop is sought out by a news agency because in the Church as a social institution he has aparently a status and authority compar-able to the managing director of some business firm. But do not mistake my point. We need not regret all this *unless* it is the only kind of authority which the Church possesses. For then the Church would be secular indeed.

As I have said, this is undoubtedly the view of the authority of the Church which many of our contemporaries hold. They would acknowledge its primary authority as a social group, though this authority is something which some of them long to diminish if not to destroy. As a secondary authority, however, the Church hardly exists for them precisely because for one reason or another they reject as either bogus or irrelevant the claims of the facts which they suppose it exists to purvey and perpetuate.

Our discussion suggests that Christians have two lessons to learn from this interpretation of the authority of the Church, or perhaps the two lessons are the negative and positive sides of the same lesson.

(*a*) Let us be alert to the mistake of supposing that the only primary authority is facts, regarded as solid, independent things which pro-vide us with the final basis for belief and action. If we make that mistake, we shall not only be inadequate in our view of the Church, we shall hardly have the right to be called religious. The authority of the Church must at least involve reference to the conceptual scheme which accompanies the facts, and this scheme will certainly have a further and distinctive point to make, a point which goes beyond those "facts" as such.

(*b*) While the Church is obviously, if only in part, a secular group and while for that very reason it will possess some degree of authority in contemporary society, we must make it evident that like the saint, the Church is only distinctively herself when she displays "saintly authority". This is something we discern and acknowledge in a saint even when his physical and intellectual condition is relatively poverty-stricken. Not that this is any excuse for the saint or the Church being content with what is physically and intellectually second-rate.

All of this brings us to the other view of the authority of the Church. On this view and by contrast, the Church is not a transmitter of facts but a token, a sign, and a symbol of God's activity in Jesus Christ where, as it is commonly expressed, the sign is part of what is signified, and the symbol part of what is symbolized. Authority inheres in the Church, as it may inhere in the Moral Law or the person. Indeed, it is significant that the model of the Church most appropriate to this concept of authority has been the "Body of Christ" — the Church, like our Lord's human body expressing the activity of God which is the Gospel. In a parallel way, the authority of the Bible is the authority of the "Word of God" which inheres in it. It is not surprising then that in the English Ordinal when the priest, by the laying on of hands, is given an authoritative rôle in the Church — so that an authority inheres in him, as in an ambassador, a prime minister, and so on — his authority is that of the Holy Spirit: "Receive the Holy Ghost for the office and work of a Priest in the Church of God", and that he also expresses in words his acceptance of the authority of the "Word of God", and is given a copy of the Bible by the Bishop. So Bible and Church are no longer transmitters of authority but are themselves tokens, symbols, and expressions of it. Each, so to say, is a projection, a slant on what each in its own way contrives to express, and both are needed — with much else — for the best understanding of what God did in Jesus of Nazareth: what has been diversely called by the phrases we mentioned on pp. 71-2 above.

Since Bible and Church are not now secondary authorities, they are not rightly pictured as channels or pipe-lines for something quite different from themselves. No question now arises as to whether one or the other could be dispensed with. On this view neither is infallible. But authoritarianism can be displayed around both when those who acknowledge the authoritative claim of either, associate with that claim only one possible interpretation, which they suppose to be self-guaranteed — or as they would more often put it, guaranteed by God. But this in effect is again to confound what is disclosed with our understanding of it.

Quite apart, however, from the logical howlers to which this view may lead, there are two hazards which in the present age specially beset this view of the authority of the Church.

The first is the supposition that this kind of spiritual authority is so precious and distinctive that it becomes empirically irrelevant, so that the Church does not speak to a secular man any word which he can understand. On this view of its authority, the Church is so anxious to disclaim the authority of a social group, and to claim transcendence, that it becomes irrelevant to contemporary society. It is tempted to stay in what it supposes to be the ivory tower of disclosures, busy in theological word-spinning and oblivious to what is going on outside.

The second hazard is that since this view eschews infallibilities, the authority of the Church does not translate into those authoritative pronouncements about problems of belief or behaviour which so many seek. The Church then seems to lack any authority at all because it gives no clear definite answers. Those who make this complaint seldom stop, however, to think that an inordinate affection for authoritative pronouncements may be verbal idolatry, since the best examples we know of infallible assertions, for example, "the cat is on the mat", are, like Russell's protocol sentences, devoid of that very transcendent reference which is needful to make them religious. Which only shows what a muddle thought in this area can generate.

Taking these two hazards along with the lessons we were to learn from the earlier view, I conclude with two major points:

(*a*) The Church may have authority as a social institution and there is certainly no credit to it if its secular wisdom is inferior to that of the children of this world. But whatever its authority as a social group, the authority it must never fail to display is the authority which belongs to God's activity in Jesus Christ. Nor must it ever exercise this distinctive authority as though it were the authority which belongs to a secular society — even though it has made this mistake in days past. Was there not a time when religious conformity could appeal to the compelling power of the Magistrate, though it is to the credit of an empiricist like Locke that, wiser than his empirical colleagues, he saw that civil power and grace are not logical kinsmen. We must not condemn the Church for being secular : and the Church must also be spiritually authoritative. But we can, and must, condemn the Church for interpreting spiritual authority in secular terms.

The first need of the Church to-day is to mediate an authoritative vision, to lead the world beyond the "facts" which for so many are reality — all that there is. The Church must so exhibit its disclosure authority that men see in it God's activity in Christ. But how will the Church lead men to this vision in our own time? How will the Church recapture the only sort of authority to which it can lay special claim? These questions bring me to my second point : which may be seen as some attempt, however inadequate, to answer the question with which Professor Kinder concluded his paper.

(*b*) My answer, ironically enough, is that the Church must learn a new secularism.

In its theology and literature, the Church has its own traditional expressions of the authority which it exhibits. Let it bring these alongside the problems of our contemporary society to see where the one matches the other. To a management troubled by the selection of personnel by psychological techniques, not least when these conflict with selection by personal interview; to the executive who sees himself caught in the rat-race where every production target is replaced by a higher one as soon as it is reached; to all who find even the most affluent society deeply unsatisfying — let theology lead out its discourse about man, eschatology, abundant life respectively, until each discovers points at which their languages match. In this way, theology will learn a new interlocking with that society of which all of us — Christians or not — are members; from its own problems contemporary society may thus be led to the authoritative vision and the Church will regain its authority within that society, discovering at the same time that it has revitalized its theology.

I am well aware that this is a very different account of the authority

and task of the Church from that which is often given. It is sometimes said that because the revelation in Jesus Christ is final, then
not only has his teaching absolute authority, but the Church and
the Bible as inspired by Jesus Christ have an authority which is
that of Jesus himself. Hence, it is argued, Church and Bible have
an infallibility which makes possible the feeding of definite teaching
to the hungry sheep. Even if this view did not confound authority
and infallibility and did not confuse primary and secondary
authorities, we should still rightly criticize it for making Christians
precisely like sheep, and certainly not free human beings responsible
and intelligent.

In a different vein altogether, we have seen earlier that the
authority of the Church will never have an infallible expression and
that an authoritarianism which runs to death one possible expression is indefensible. The Church's authoritative challenge is one
which will always be linked with fallibility. But this is no weakness.
It enables the Church to see where her treasure really lies; it gives
her an authority which like that of the Moral Law can be associated
with personal freedom and integrity and it leads to a constructive
and appropriate involvement in contemporary society.

The Church will never regain her authority in contemporary
society until she has seen better that her authority is the compelling
authority of a vision of God's love which she herself in her life must
express; and until, in humility, she has struggled to relate her
theology with the problems of thought and action which she has
learned by listening to what secular men have had to say. A Church
characterized by such vision and humility would have an authority
of the kind which can never arise around a Church which saw herself as a purveyor of hard facts and well-polished infallibilities. As
Dr Schmidt said, the Church must be a disturber of man's com-
placency. Only when a Church is characterized by vision and
humility will men recognize in her the sure presence of her Lord
to whom, as Dr Käsemann and others have reminded us, we must
bear witness in self-sacrificing service, which of course includes the
service and suffering which is involved in all explorations of
thought and wrestling with problems.

SUMMARY

I have been concerned to show that the concept of authority occurs in at least two fairly well defined contexts. One of these centres on "facts" to which a nodding assent is appropriate, or more accurately on facts within a conceptual scheme, which is associated with an intellectual commitment; the other context arises around what we have called a disclosure situation such as occurs when we discern intuitively an authority inhering in the Moral Law or a person, and to which we freely respond.

We first saw that there can be no belief on evidence which altogether avoids an appeal to authority, though this is then an appeal to what is conveniently called a secondary authority—that by which the primary authority, in this case facts, is transmitted. I argued, however, that this appeal to facts, if rightly and adequately understood, also involves commitment to a conceptual scheme, and as a primary authority is closer to another kind of primary authority than might have seemed to be the case at first sight.

The second kind of primary authority is that kind of authority which inheres in the Moral Law or in a person. To make a spontaneous response to such an authority is to realize our freedom and status as persons. On this general background we argued first for the reasonableness of an appeal to authority, and then that an appeal to authority does not necessarily compromise our intellectual integrity, because in the first context we have access to the evidence ourselves, and in the second context there is always the task of explication to be done. Only if this is denied do we get authoritarianism, and unjust claims for infallibility .

The implication of all this for the authority of the Church is that there are broadly two accounts which may be given of it. The Church is bound to possess, in a higher or lower degree and for better or worse, the authority of a social group and to be a secondary, transmitting authority for Christian "facts". But it must also possess—and this distinctively—the authority of a transcendent challenge. It is this second kind of authority which it can so often fail to display; it is this which our contemporary society can well fail to discern. Certainly, to possess and to communicate this authority is undoubtedly our greatest contemporary task. In relation to Professor Kinder's challenging question, I made only one practical suggestion as to how we might do this—namely, engaging with all men of good will—believers or not—on the stubborn problems of thought and behaviour which confront us all. A final warning: we must beware of contemporary society expecting from us the kind of authority which would express itself in terms of infallible pronouncements. Such authority is not to be found in the logic of religious thought or behaviour, and for the Church to try to have it, will always be disastrous—at least in the long run.

DISCUSSION

DISCUSSION on Canon Ramsey's paper was opened by Dr
W. Schweitzer, who said:

I must admit that Canon Ramsey's contribution left me at first in
a state of confusion: on the one hand the problem of authority is
treated philosophically in a manner with which I am not very
familiar; this covers the greater part of his paper. When I was
reading this part for the second time it began to fascinate me. Yet
the question still remained—and this is the other side of the matter
—what this had to do with theology, with the authority of the
Church. But then came the great surprise: the last part of the paper
contained a number of assertions to which I can well subscribe,
although Canon Ramsey reached his conclusions by a route very
different from what I had expected. Incidentally, this experience
often occurs in ecumenical conversations.

Now to some particular observations:

1. *Method.* I fully agree with the use of contemporary philosophy
in the field of theological thought in order to control our use of
language, our terminology, our thought-forms. We are all philosophers—from the moment we open our mouths. However, we ought
to beware lest there is only one-way traffic: there should be traffic
in both directions. It may well happen that the philosopher asks
questions which simply do not fit in with the theologian's subject-
matter. (At Morning Prayer yesterday, Canon Ramsey himself read
Genesis 3: doubtless the serpent there puts a question which we
must refuse to admit, "hath God said . . . ?")

2. *Result.* The result of Canon Ramsey's philosophical deliberations
may be summarized thus: "Beware of 'authoritarianism' and of all
claims to infallibility." Excellent! The question I now ask is the
following: Is this also theologically relevant? Must this warning
be expressed even more sharply in theological terms under certain
circumstances? We have to investigate why we as theologians cannot in fact avoid these challenges that are simultaneously "linked
with fallibility".[8]

---

8 P. 78 above.

3. *Authority*. The very word "authority" is to be challenged. We all say, of course, that Christ is our "authority" but this he is precisely by calling himself our servant, that is one who has no authority. He is the *Son* of the Father. In the same way the apostles called themselves "slaves", ministers; indeed, the heart of God's action in Jesus Christ is that he laid aside his authority so that he could be with us, with his people, with our weakness and loneliness. Ultimately the manner of God's action warns us against accepting the term "authority" in its usual meaning. When theologians use this or a similar term or image, they can do so only if they attempt to clothe these terms and images with new meaning in the light of God's action; and only then will it become meaningful to use the term authority.

4. *The expectation of modern society*. This is the real reason why the Church must disappoint contemporary society when it expects her to be able to make infallible pronouncements.[9] We must try and make our contemporaries understand that this is precisely what we are absolutely forbidden to offer them. The world always expects the truth to be comprehensible in a series of statements; we must insist that the truth of God is always "truth in encounter".[10] By offering infallible pronouncements we encourage men to hanker after security — an object of Luther's frequent attack. The world always wants security: by yielding to this demand the Church becomes a kind of insurance agency. Men want us to confirm their natural desires (for example, the refugees in Germany *expect* the Church to support their desire to return to their lost homes in the East). We cannot offer these securities, we can only point to this: it is a risk to believe in Christ and to follow him, and no authority can help men to avoid that risk. In taking this risk man can attain the assurance of faith; this assurance of faith is something very different from the security of reason.

5. *The authority of the Church*. The Church's authority is based on her going forth into the world as the handmaid of men to invite them to the Lord's Table. It is the same to-day as it has always been or at any rate always should have been. The invitation says: Take the risk, follow Christ!

---

9 Cf. p. 78 above.
10 Cf. the well-known title of E. Brunner's book.

Even the Church of Rome has now begun to climb down from her throne: Leo XIII and Pius XI still spoke of the Church as the judge of social problems. John XXIII, on the other hand, called her only *Mater et magistra*. Better still, the Church should call herself *ancilla hominis et societatis*. This is her true position in the world, and this may then be called a "saintly authority".[11]

6. *The handmaid of society*. The Church as the *ancilla societatis* is sent (*missio*) into the world for service (διακονία). She must therefore concern herself with men's real problems, both individual and social. In doing this she must accept and even develop a "new secularism".[12] She should not make general statements about right conduct, but help men in concrete situations to come to a decision "in the Mind of Christ"; there is no department of life where we are not in need of justification and sanctification through him.[13] All this has no other purpose than to call men to faith, to invite them to follow Christ, to point to him, even in suffering to bear witness to his Name, the Name of the crucified Lord.

7. *The Church's authority regained?* Should we expect the Church to regain a kind of authority?[14] I would contest this, firstly on sociological grounds. In this world we Christians are in the position of a minority and this is likely to remain so. More important, however, is the theological objection: this very situation is far more consistent than any other with the charge laid upon this group of people to be a sign of the crucified and risen Lord in the world (of the risen Lord whose Resurrection men are unable to see). The Church is a sign and manifestation of his Resurrection:[15] she points to him who is to come.

We invite men to the Lord's Table: this does not mean that we always have to be talking about eschatology (as Canon Ramsey put it in one place), much less that we should force a particular eschatology on our fellow-men. It is enough for us that we serve men, and that some will then accept our service as a sign of his

11 P. 77 above.
12 Cf. p. 79 above.
13 Cf. Declaration of Barmen, point 2.
14 P. 79 above.
15 Cf. p. 77 above.

hidden service. And when we have done all that was our duty, we should say: "We are unprofitable servants..."

The Church will achieve her authority as a servant in so far as she is ready to give herself for the sake of the world. If she does that, then she may be sure that she will not lose her life but that she will be kept alive through her Lord who alone holds authority over the future.

[Full discussion of the points raised by Professor Schweitzer was held over until later, since all the members of the Conference then left to attend a reception and luncheon at the Mitre Hotel, Oxford, at which the host was the Bishop of Oxford, the Right Reverend Harry Carpenter, D.D.]

FURTHER DISCUSSION was opened by Canon C. F. D. Moule, who said:

Perhaps it will not be amiss if I start by attempting a very brief outline of the first part of Canon Ramsey's paper.

He began by observing that, in view of the large variety of ways in which the word "authority" is used, it would be salutary to follow Wittgenstein's slogan, "Don't look for meanings, look for use"—which Canon Ramsey interpreted as "being alert to *contexts*". Two contexts, he said, would (at least *prima facie*) become distinguishable, with quite different metaphysical presuppositions; and, although these presuppositions need not be incompatible, the one preferred by contemporary society is that with which it is least possible to do justice to the Church as a religious community. (He meant the presupposition that "facts", so called, are sacred.)

By way of helping us to be alert to contexts, he noted three pairs of contrasts:

(*a*) Between belief on evidence and belief on authority;
(*b*) Between primary and secondary authorities;
(*c*) Between the authority of a "fact" and the authority of a person.

But, when these are examined, it turns out that none of them is as obvious as at first appeared. In (*a*), even the most obvious sort of "belief on evidence" (for example, by scientific experiment) contains *some* element of "belief on authority"; and *vice versa*. In (*b*) the distinction between so-called "facts" as primary, and, as secondary, all the "transmitting agents", turns out to be fallacious, because—(c)—it is becoming increasingly clear that it is impossible to isolate a "fact" from its context and the personal factor. "There are no basic facts" (J. R. Lucas); what we have to look for is not "facts" but whatever it is that calls from us faith in, or commitment to, a certain understanding of the universe (R. M. Hare).

Thus, we are led to recognize that authority often inheres in a *person* as active in a certain rôle; and when a person is a primary authority, this authority is "intuited in a vision" or "declared in a disclosure"—the disclosure being of the person's *transcendence*.

Canon Ramsey ended this section with two observations:

(a) In various ways, an appeal to authority runs through the whole pattern of belief and behaviour, and is reasonable, precisely in being so widespread and ubiquitous.

(b) An appeal to authority need not compromise freedom (except for those who "worship" facts!); neither is authority the same as infallibility; and therefore, the appeal to authority need not be authoritarian.

There are many questions of detail I should like to ask here; but, instead, let me offer some more general observations.

If this part of Canon Ramsey's paper seemed, to some of us, alien, this was perhaps because some of us sharply distinguish the realms of philosophy and theology. This distinction was evident in some of Dr Schweitzer's questions this morning.[16] But I think it is characteristic of Anglican theology that it tries to see life (including thought) as *whole* and indivisible. (This, no doubt, has something to do with the Anglican respect for the reasonable, which has come up from time to time in these discussions.)

If then one tries not to departmentalize, one comes more naturally from Canon Ramsey's first part to his second—the relevance of his discussion of authority in general to the Church's authority in particular.

If we are to make any contact with the secular world, it must be by claiming that God *is* already there, and by letting him *show* himself there through the Church—the Church as "a token, sign, and symbol" of God's activity in Jesus Christ.

16 P. 83 above.

This is another way of saying what is said in the second part, that the Church should not make the mistake of claiming the sort of transcendence which excuses it from trying to make itself intelligible to the ordinary man.

I would also like to add, by way of comment, that this mistake is precisely what was killed dead in the death of Christ. Jesus did speak to "secular man", by his rejection of security and his willingness to serve without reservation: the σκάνδαλον in Christ was not obscurity but intolerable clarity. He did make intelligible and terrifyingly clear what God is like—and human nature rejected it.

And I believe that Church's "voice" is heard by the secular world whenever it is uttered (not only in words but in deeds) in terms of making man whole. This involves leading men to faith in Christ and to full *manhood* in him. For the Gospel of the Incarnation is about *man* ("What is man?") as well as about God: about man's true manhood as consisting in the worship of God. It is a Gospel of *imago dei*. (It is significant that, in the New Testament context and against an Hebraic background, εἰκών is almost the same as δόξα; reflecting God's glory is precisely man's function; and to help man into it is the Church's task.)

This leads straight back to a question raised in a previous discussion—the relation of Christ to creation. Would it be true to say that, just as the only distinctively Christian conception of *God* is in terms of the Cross (he is the God and Father of our Lord Jesus Christ), so, equally, the only distinctively Christian conception of *creation* is also in terms of the Cross? Is the principle of creation, of cosmology, to be found in self-limitation, self-giving, the taking of risks? Did God limit himself and expose himself to risks to *make* the κόσμος, just as he did, and does, to remake it? If so, then the familiar fact that soteriology goes hand-in-hand with cosmology in New Testament christology is due to the profoundest possible organic connection between the two.

So, at last, we return to the matter of authority. The only authority that the Church can claim is not that of *Mater magistra* but of *ancilla* (so Dr Schweitzer this morning [17]), precisely because this is the only *creative* authority and the only authority that can be recognized and freely accepted by man—man who is created in

[17] P. 85 above.

God's image and is, under God, responsible for authority over creation.

On this showing, the Church, by recalling man *by* service *to* obedient service, is meant to restore man to his position of *responsible authority* in the universe (cf. Ps. 8; Rom. 8; 1 Cor. 15; Heb. 2). Man's proper authority (as εἰκὼν θεοῦ) is the authority of obedient responsibility; and this, though not "infallible" is something of which we may, and must be absolutely convinced.

* There has, I think, been very close agreement between us in this Conference (in principle—however often we may forget it) about authority not being *propositional*,[18] and about its being not *imperium* but *dominium*; perhaps this *dominium* needs now to be more consciously worked out in terms of a doctrine of man.

FOLLOWING Canon Moule's remarks, a general agreement was quickly reached that in Christ God meets us in clarity, not obscurity; he revealed the will of God so palpably as to make it a σκάνδαλον. Mention of the offence caused by Christ and also by his followers [19] provoked a good deal of discussion on the authority of preaching. Men did not understand God in his wisdom, and it pleased God to save men through the μωρία of Christ crucified (1 Cor. 1); so how can the Church in the present day claim to be the bearer of a credible message? The Word is infallible, and the Word preached can claim infallibility. The authority of the apostle is that of an οἰκονόμος. The Conference was reminded that Luther said he did not ask for forgiveness after having delivered a sermon. In the words of one German delegate, the preaching of the Word rightly and with assurance implied *haec dixit Dominus* and Jesus' own *ego dixi*. Whilst we must eschew the claim of infallibility for the Church's ministers, we must equally hold fast to our *certitudo loquendi*.[20] An English delegate questioned whether the identification with Christ was so complete in the case of preaching as it was in the case of the sacrament of the Eucharist, and it was agreed that it may be better to speak of Christ identifying himself with the Church as a whole rather than with isolated activities within

18 See pp. 10-12.
19 See also p. 53 above.
20 Cf. Bishop Butler's doctrine of probability and Newman's doctrine of certitude.

the life of the Church. It was agreed that this whole topic would merit full-scale discussion in the future.

The need to work out the Christian concept of authority in terms of the doctrine of Man was discussed further. "Facts" which are treated as objects and leave aside entirely the subjective element fall short of fully personal authority; authority must be that of a person, and not of mere facts, since the authority of a person engages those confronted in a response. The Church is gripped by the authority of Christ and similarly the Church must be the dynamic reflection of Christ's authority, who both mirrors the fatherly heart of God and makes men whole by restoring them to their true image of God. However, in the life of the Church a distinction needs to be made between the authority attaching to the person of a Christian minister as representing Christ and the authority of the divine gift conveyed by him. The authority of the person must always stand in the shadow of the Cross and reflect the true image of the Cross; the divine gift, all were agreed, remained unimpaired by human failures.[21]

What is a fact? In discussion on this point, raised originally in Canon Ramsey's paper, a distinction emerged between two kinds of fact : on the one hand, brute facts (*bruta facta*) are ambiguous and have no authority by themselves; on the other hand, facts involving a relationship or personal attitude may become authoritative in virtue of the personal element attaching to them. Mere factuality is of significance only if by this we mean what is given and cannot be reversed. The philosophical statement in Canon Ramsey's paper that it is the reasonable man who creates facts would find its theological equivalent in the statement that the faithful man is one who acknowledges all given facts, including of

---

[21] Cf. Article XXVI, "Of the Unworthiness of the Ministers, which hinders not the effect of the Sacrament".

course the facts about God's self-disclosure in Christ. Berkeley said that brute facts led to atheism.

Canon Ramsey was given the opportunity to reply briefly and said:

(*a*) He certainly rejected the so-called "sense-data" of Bertrand Russell — that is, static brute facts, detached and independent.

(*b*) We are confronted by facts surrounded by their context.

(*c*) Authority is personal.

(*d*) God's activity in Christ is an essential part of the data before us.

Many people to-day asked whether the existence of God was a matter of fact, and as regards the relationship between philosophy and theology it must be said that all questions were fitting for theology. Philosophy may serve as the handmaid of theology, and this too is the function of metaphysics when once suitably chastened.

BIBLIOGRAPHY

The Chairman of the Conference brought a number of books as samples of work produced on the subject of the Conference in the English language. The books were:

A. SABATIER, *The Religions of Authority and the Religion of the Spirit*, Williams and Norgate, 1899.

JOHN OMAN, *Vision and Authority*, Hodder and Stoughton, 1902.

P. T. FORSYTH, *The Principle of Authority*, Hodder and Stoughton, 1913.

Essays Catholic and Critical, S.P.C.K., 1926.

C. H. DODD, *The Authority of the Bible*, Nisbet, 1928.

C. F. GARBETT, *Authority in Doctrine*, S.P.C.K., 1950.

R. R. WILLIAMS, *Authority in the Apostolic Age*, S.C.M., 1950.

ALAN RICHARDSON and WOLFGANG SCHWEITZER, *Biblical Authority for To-day*, S.C.M., 1951.

J. K. S. REID, *The Authority of Scripture*, Methuen, 1957.

JOHN KENNEDY, *Presbyterian Authority and Discipline*, St Andrew's Press, 1960.

A. M. RAMSEY, *The Authority of the Bible*, Nelson and Sons, 1962.

J. M. TODD, *Problems of Authority*, Darton, Longman and Todd, 1962. (Paperback edition 1964.)

PUBLISHER'S NOTE

S.P.C.K. THEOLOGICAL COLLECTIONS

The purpose of this series is to bring together in convenient and accessible form some of the occasional work of contemporary theologians on selected themes of particular interest or importance. This present volume is the account of a single conference, but most numbers contain contributions which, although intended to illuminate a common theme, were originally written independently and approach their theme in quite different ways. Some material contained in the volumes of *Theological Collections* has been reprinted from periodicals or elsewhere and some has not hitherto been published; but the fact that these contributions have been put together into this form means that they are thought to be of more than ephemeral value. Details of other volumes in this series are given below.

Vol. 1   *On the Authority of the Bible*

        Leonard Hodgson, C. F. Evans, John Burnaby,
        Gerhard Ebeling, D. E. Nineham.

        1960. 104 pp. 8s. 6d.

Vol. 2   *The Communication of the Gospel in New Testament Times*

        Austin Farrer, C. F. Evans, J. A. Emerton,
        F. W. Beare, R. A. Markus, F. W. Dillistone.

        1961. 96 pp. 8s. 6d.

Vol. 3   *The Miracles and the Resurrection*
        I. T. Ramsey, G. H. Boobyer, F. N. Davey,
        M. C. Perry, Henry J. Cadbury.

        1964. 112 pp. 13s. 6d.

Vol. 4	*The Authorship and Integrity of the New Testament*

Kurt Aland, Donald Guthrie, A. Q. Morton,
J. A. T. Robinson, G. Bornkamm, A. M. G. Stephenson,
Massey H. Shepherd, Jr.

1965. 120 pp. 15s. 6d.

Vol. 6	*Historicity and Chronology in the New Testament*

September 1965. 168 pp. 17s. 6d.

How far do we have, in the narrative sections of the New Testament (and in particular in the Gospels) an historically reliable account of actual happenings; and how far may we legitimately ask chronological questions of our material? After a period of historical scepticism, these questions are being asked again, but never in the same sort of way. The aim of the essays in this volume (almost all of them newly written) is to provide students—not necessarily professional scholars—with a conspectus of recent study and to make some contribution to the ongoing debate.

Contributors:

D. E. Nineham, Allan Barr, C. S. Mann,
A. R. C. Leaney, H. E. W. Turner, George Ogg,
A. N. Sherwin-White, William Lillie,
A. M. Ramsey, R. R. Williams.

2027X